**TEACHER'S PET PUBLICATIONS**

PUZZLE PACK
for
Their Eyes Were Watching God

based on the book by
Zora Neale Hurston

Written by
William T. Collins

© 2005 Teacher's Pet Publications
All Rights Reserved

The materials in this packet are copyrighted
by Teacher's Pet Publications, Inc.

These pages may be duplicated by the purchaser
for use in the purchaser's own classroom.

Copying any of these materials and distributing them
for any other purpose is a violation of the copyright laws.

© 2005 Teacher's Pet Publications, Inc.
www.tpet.com

INTRODUCTION
If you already own the LitPlan for this title, this Puzzle Pack will refresh your Unit Resource Materials and Vocabulary Resource Materials sections plus give you additional materials you can substitute into the tests. If you do not already have a complete LitPlan, these pages will give you some supplemental materials to use with your own plan. There are two main groups of materials: one set for unit words (such as characters' names, symbols, places, etc.) and one set for vocabulary words associated with the book.

WORD LIST
There is a word list for both the unit words and the vocabulary words. These lists show you which words are being used in the materials and the clues or definitions being used for those words. You may want to give students a word list with clues/definitions to help them, or you may want students to only have a word list (without clues/definitions) if you want them to work a little harder. Both are available for duplication. The word lists can also be your "calling key" for the bingo games.

FILL IN THE BLANK AND MATCHING
There are 4 each of the fill in the blank and matching worksheets for both the unit and vocabulary words. These pages can be used either as extra worksheets for students or as objective parts of a unit test. They can be done individually if students need extra help or as a whole class activity to review the material covered.

MAGIC SQUARES
The magic squares not only reinforce the material covered but also work on reasoning and math skills. Many teachers have told us that their students really enjoy doing these!

WORD SEARCH PUZZLES
The word search words go in all directions, as indicated on your answer keys. Two of the word search puzzles have the clues listed rather than the words. This makes the puzzle a little more difficult, but it reinforces the material better. Two word search puzzles have words only for students who find the clue puzzles too difficult.

CROSSWORD PUZZLES
Both unit and vocabulary word sections have 4 crossword puzzles.

BINGO CARDS
There are 32 individual bingo cards for the unit words and 32 individual bingo cards for the vocabulary words. You can use your word list as a "call list," calling the words at random and marking them off of your list as you go, or you could use the flash cards by cutting them apart and drawing the words at random from a hat (or box or whatever). To make a better review, you might ask for the definition and spelling of each word as you call it out–or you could call out the definitions and have students tell you the words they need to look for on the puzzle.

JUGGLE LETTERS
The vocabulary juggle letter game is intended to help students learn the spellings of the words. One sheet has the definitions listed on it as an extra help for students who need it or to reinforce the definitions if you choose to do so.

FLASH CARDS
We've included a set of vocabulary flash cards you can duplicate, cut, and fold for your students. Some teachers make a few sets for general use by the class; others make a set for each student. Some teachers duplicate them for each student and have the students cut & fold their own. You can cut out just the words and put them in a hat, have each student pick out one word and write the definition and a sentence for that word. Students then swap words and papers, with the next student adding a sentence of his own under the last one. You can have students swap as many times as you like. Each time the student will read the sentences written prior to his own and then add a sentence. You can cut out the words and definitions separately and play "I Have; Who Has?" Each student in the room draws a word and definition. The first student says, "I have (the name of the word). Who has the definition?" The student with the definition reads it then says, "I have (the name of the vocabulary word she has). Who has the definition?" The round continues until all words and definitions have been given.

Their Eyes Were Watching God Word List

No.	Word	Clue/Definition
1.	BEANS	Crop they picked on the muck
2.	BOOTYNY	Threw his coffee cup at Coodemay
3.	CAKE	Tea ____
4.	COODEMAY	Tea Cake tried to put him out of the restaurant
5.	DOG	Tea Cake killed it to save Janie
6.	EATONVILLE	Town where Joe and Janie settled
7.	EVERGLADES	Location of the muck
8.	GAMBLING	How Tea Cake got Janie's money back
9.	HAIR	Janie's most noticeable physical characteristic
10.	HEADACHE	Tea Cake's first symptom
11.	HEADRAGS	Joe made Janie wear them in the store
12.	HEZEKIAH	Acted like Joe in the store
13.	HURRICANE	Caused evacuation of the muck
14.	JACKSONVILLE	Site of Tea Cake and Janie's wedding
15.	JANIE	Narrator of the story
16.	JODY	Joe's nickname
17.	JOE	Janie's businessman-mayor husband
18.	KILLICKS	Last name of Janie's farmer husband
19.	LAMP	Town celebrated its installation; street ____
20.	LOGAN	Mr. Killicks' first name
21.	MAYOR	Joe was the first one in Eatonville
22.	MOTORBOAT	Slept through the hurricane
23.	MOURNING	It shouldn't last any longer than grief
24.	MUCK	What Tea Cake called the Everglade crop land
25.	MULE	Nanny compared the black woman to one
26.	NANNY	Raised Janie
27.	NUNKIE	Made a play for Tea Cake
28.	OKECHOBEE	Overflowing lake
29.	PHOEBY	First to hear Janie's story
30.	PISTOL	Tea Cake's weapon
31.	RABIES	Disease Tea Cake got from dog
32.	RIFLE	Janie's weapon
33.	SEEDS	Janie brought these back from the muck
34.	SEMINOLES	Janie watched a band of them leave the muck
35.	SERRENT	Drunken instigator of fight at the restaurant
36.	SIMMONS	Doctor who testified in Janie's behalf
37.	SOP	Wanted to testify at Janie's trial: ____-de-Bottom
38.	STORE	Joe started one in Eatonville
39.	SWALLOW	What Tea Cake couldn't do when he was sick
40.	TRIAL	Held the same day as Tea Cake's death
41.	TURNER	Mrs. ____ didn't like dark-skinned Blacks
42.	WOODS	Vergible ____; Tea Cake

Their Eyes Were Watching God Fill In The Blanks 1

_____ 1. Caused evacuation of the muck
_____ 2. Janie's weapon
_____ 3. Tea ____
_____ 4. Janie watched a band of them leave the muck
_____ 5. Janie brought these back from the muck
_____ 6. Town celebrated its installation; street ___
_____ 7. What Tea Cake called the Everglade crop land
_____ 8. Tea Cake's first symptom
_____ 9. Joe started one in Eatonville
_____ 10. Mr. Killicks' first name
_____ 11. Site of Tea Cake and Janie's wedding
_____ 12. Location of the muck
_____ 13. Last name of Janie's farmer husband
_____ 14. Town where Joe and Janie settled
_____ 15. Nanny compared the black woman to one
_____ 16. Drunken instigator of fight at the restaurant
_____ 17. Slept through the hurricane
_____ 18. Wanted to testify at Janie's trial: ___-de-Bottom
_____ 19. Joe made Janie wear them in the store
_____ 20. First to hear Janie's story

Their Eyes Were Watching God Fill In The Blanks 1 Answer Key

HURRICANE	1. Caused evacuation of the muck
RIFLE	2. Janie's weapon
CAKE	3. Tea ___
SEMINOLES	4. Janie watched a band of them leave the muck
SEEDS	5. Janie brought these back from the muck
LAMP	6. Town celebrated its installation; street ___
MUCK	7. What Tea Cake called the Everglade crop land
HEADACHE	8. Tea Cake's first symptom
STORE	9. Joe started one in Eatonville
LOGAN	10. Mr. Killicks' first name
JACKSONVILLE	11. Site of Tea Cake and Janie's wedding
EVERGLADES	12. Location of the muck
KILLICKS	13. Last name of Janie's farmer husband
EATONVILLE	14. Town where Joe and Janie settled
MULE	15. Nanny compared the black woman to one
SERRENT	16. Drunken instigator of fight at the restaurant
MOTORBOAT	17. Slept through the hurricane
SOP	18. Wanted to testify at Janie's trial: ___-de-Bottom
HEADRAGS	19. Joe made Janie wear them in the store
PHOEBY	20. First to hear Janie's story

Their Eyes Were Watching God Fill In The Blanks 2

_____ 1. Drunken instigator of fight at the restaurant
_____ 2. Joe was the first one in Eatonville
_____ 3. It shouldn't last any longer than grief
_____ 4. Doctor who testified in Janie's behalf
_____ 5. Janie brought these back from the muck
_____ 6. Joe's nickname
_____ 7. First to hear Janie's story
_____ 8. Mrs. ___ didn't like dark-skinned Blacks
_____ 9. Tea Cake tried to put him out of the restaurant
_____ 10. Janie watched a band of them leave the muck
_____ 11. What Tea Cake couldn't do when he was sick
_____ 12. Site of Tea Cake and Janie's wedding
_____ 13. Threw his coffee cup at Coodemay
_____ 14. Town celebrated its installation; street ___
_____ 15. Town where Joe and Janie settled
_____ 16. Janie's businessman-mayor husband
_____ 17. Held the same day as Tea Cake's death
_____ 18. How Tea Cake got Janie's money back
_____ 19. Made a play for Tea Cake
_____ 20. Raised Janie

Their Eyes Were Watching God Fill In The Blanks 2 Answer Key

SERRENT	1. Drunken instigator of fight at the restaurant
MAYOR	2. Joe was the first one in Eatonville
MOURNING	3. It shouldn't last any longer than grief
SIMMONS	4. Doctor who testified in Janie's behalf
SEEDS	5. Janie brought these back from the muck
JODY	6. Joe's nickname
PHOEBY	7. First to hear Janie's story
TURNER	8. Mrs. ___ didn't like dark-skinned Blacks
COODEMAY	9. Tea Cake tried to put him out of the restaurant
SEMINOLES	10. Janie watched a band of them leave the muck
SWALLOW	11. What Tea Cake couldn't do when he was sick
JACKSONVILLE	12. Site of Tea Cake and Janie's wedding
BOOTYNY	13. Threw his coffee cup at Coodemay
LAMP	14. Town celebrated its installation; street ___
EATONVILLE	15. Town where Joe and Janie settled
JOE	16. Janie's businessman-mayor husband
TRIAL	17. Held the same day as Tea Cake's death
GAMBLING	18. How Tea Cake got Janie's money back
NUNKIE	19. Made a play for Tea Cake
NANNY	20. Raised Janie

Their Eyes Were Watching God Fill In The Blanks 3

_____ 1. Town celebrated its installation; street ___

_____ 2. Joe's nickname

_____ 3. Town where Joe and Janie settled

_____ 4. Last name of Janie's farmer husband

_____ 5. Janie brought these back from the muck

_____ 6. Site of Tea Cake and Janie's wedding

_____ 7. First to hear Janie's story

_____ 8. Threw his coffee cup at Coodemay

_____ 9. Wanted to testify at Janie's trial: ___-de-Bottom

_____ 10. Location of the muck

_____ 11. Caused evacuation of the muck

_____ 12. Joe started one in Eatonville

_____ 13. Janie watched a band of them leave the muck

_____ 14. Raised Janie

_____ 15. Tea ____

_____ 16. Made a play for Tea Cake

_____ 17. Tea Cake's first symptom

_____ 18. Tea Cake's weapon

_____ 19. Janie's most noticeable physical characteristic

_____ 20. Vergible _____; Tea Cake

Their Eyes Were Watching God Fill In The Blanks 3 Answer Key

LAMP	1. Town celebrated its installation; street ___
JODY	2. Joe's nickname
EATONVILLE	3. Town where Joe and Janie settled
KILLICKS	4. Last name of Janie's farmer husband
SEEDS	5. Janie brought these back from the muck
JACKSONVILLE	6. Site of Tea Cake and Janie's wedding
PHOEBY	7. First to hear Janie's story
BOOTYNY	8. Threw his coffee cup at Coodemay
SOP	9. Wanted to testify at Janie's trial: ___-de-Bottom
EVERGLADES	10. Location of the muck
HURRICANE	11. Caused evacuation of the muck
STORE	12. Joe started one in Eatonville
SEMINOLES	13. Janie watched a band of them leave the muck
NANNY	14. Raised Janie
CAKE	15. Tea ___
NUNKIE	16. Made a play for Tea Cake
HEADACHE	17. Tea Cake's first symptom
PISTOL	18. Tea Cake's weapon
HAIR	19. Janie's most noticeable physical characteristic
WOODS	20. Vergible ___; Tea Cake

Their Eyes Were Watching God Fill In The Blanks 4

_____ 1. Janie watched a band of them leave the muck
_____ 2. Janie's most noticeable physical characteristic
_____ 3. Slept through the hurricane
_____ 4. It shouldn't last any longer than grief
_____ 5. Doctor who testified in Janie's behalf
_____ 6. Town celebrated its installation; street ___
_____ 7. What Tea Cake called the Everglade crop land
_____ 8. Disease Tea Cake got from dog
_____ 9. Joe's nickname
_____ 10. Crop they picked on the muck
_____ 11. Threw his coffee cup at Coodemay
_____ 12. Joe made Janie wear them in the store
_____ 13. Janie brought these back from the muck
_____ 14. Drunken instigator of fight at the restaurant
_____ 15. Joe started one in Eatonville
_____ 16. Vergible _____; Tea Cake
_____ 17. Nanny compared the black woman to one
_____ 18. Tea Cake tried to put him out of the restaurant
_____ 19. Held the same day as Tea Cake's death
_____ 20. Joe was the first one in Eatonville

Their Eyes Were Watching God Fill In The Blanks 4 Answer Key

SEMINOLES	1. Janie watched a band of them leave the muck
HAIR	2. Janie's most noticeable physical characteristic
MOTORBOAT	3. Slept through the hurricane
MOURNING	4. It shouldn't last any longer than grief
SIMMONS	5. Doctor who testified in Janie's behalf
LAMP	6. Town celebrated its installation; street ___
MUCK	7. What Tea Cake called the Everglade crop land
RABIES	8. Disease Tea Cake got from dog
JODY	9. Joe's nickname
BEANS	10. Crop they picked on the muck
BOOTYNY	11. Threw his coffee cup at Coodemay
HEADRAGS	12. Joe made Janie wear them in the store
SEEDS	13. Janie brought these back from the muck
SERRENT	14. Drunken instigator of fight at the restaurant
STORE	15. Joe started one in Eatonville
WOODS	16. Vergible _____; Tea Cake
MULE	17. Nanny compared the black woman to one
COODEMAY	18. Tea Cake tried to put him out of the restaurant
TRIAL	19. Held the same day as Tea Cake's death
MAYOR	20. Joe was the first one in Eatonville

Their Eyes Were Watching God Matching 1

___ 1. SEMINOLES   A. How Tea Cake got Janie's money back
___ 2. PHOEBY   B. Overflowing lake
___ 3. PISTOL   C. Crop they picked on the muck
___ 4. HURRICANE   D. Janie's most noticeable physical characteristic
___ 5. SEEDS   E. Vergible _____; Tea Cake
___ 6. BOOTYNY   F. Tea Cake's weapon
___ 7. JODY   G. Raised Janie
___ 8. RIFLE   H. Wanted to testify at Janie's trial: ___-de-Bottom
___ 9. KILLICKS   I. Town celebrated its installation; street ___
___10. LOGAN   J. Town where Joe and Janie settled
___11. HAIR   K. Janie's weapon
___12. MULE   L. It shouldn't last any longer than grief
___13. COODEMAY   M. Tea Cake tried to put him out of the restaurant
___14. LAMP   N. Mr. Killicks' first name
___15. HEADACHE   O. Nanny compared the black woman to one
___16. EATONVILLE   P. Joe's nickname
___17. SOP   Q. Tea Cake's first symptom
___18. WOODS   R. Disease Tea Cake got from dog
___19. BEANS   S. Last name of Janie's farmer husband
___20. GAMBLING   T. First to hear Janie's story
___21. JACKSONVILLE   U. Site of Tea Cake and Janie's wedding
___22. NANNY   V. Threw his coffee cup at Coodemay
___23. OKECHOBEE   W. Caused evacuation of the muck
___24. MOURNING   X. Janie watched a band of them leave the muck
___25. RABIES   Y. Janie brought these back from the muck

Their Eyes Were Watching God Matching 1 Answer Key

X - 1. SEMINOLES	A.	How Tea Cake got Janie's money back
T - 2. PHOEBY	B.	Overflowing lake
F - 3. PISTOL	C.	Crop they picked on the muck
W - 4. HURRICANE	D.	Janie's most noticeable physical characteristic
Y - 5. SEEDS	E.	Vergible _____; Tea Cake
V - 6. BOOTYNY	F.	Tea Cake's weapon
P - 7. JODY	G.	Raised Janie
K - 8. RIFLE	H.	Wanted to testify at Janie's trial: ___-de-Bottom
S - 9. KILLICKS	I.	Town celebrated its installation; street ___
N -10. LOGAN	J.	Town where Joe and Janie settled
D -11. HAIR	K.	Janie's weapon
O -12. MULE	L.	It shouldn't last any longer than grief
M -13. COODEMAY	M.	Tea Cake tried to put him out of the restaurant
I - 14. LAMP	N.	Mr. Killicks' first name
Q -15. HEADACHE	O.	Nanny compared the black woman to one
J - 16. EATONVILLE	P.	Joe's nickname
H -17. SOP	Q.	Tea Cake's first symptom
E - 18. WOODS	R.	Disease Tea Cake got from dog
C -19. BEANS	S.	Last name of Janie's farmer husband
A -20. GAMBLING	T.	First to hear Janie's story
U -21. JACKSONVILLE	U.	Site of Tea Cake and Janie's wedding
G -22. NANNY	V.	Threw his coffee cup at Coodemay
B -23. OKECHOBEE	W.	Caused evacuation of the muck
L - 24. MOURNING	X.	Janie watched a band of them leave the muck
R -25. RABIES	Y.	Janie brought these back from the muck

Their Eyes Were Watching God Matching 2

___ 1. GAMBLING   A. How Tea Cake got Janie's money back
___ 2. RIFLE   B. Janie's weapon
___ 3. HEADRAGS   C. Raised Janie
___ 4. MOTORBOAT   D. Mrs. ___ didn't like dark-skinned Blacks
___ 5. CAKE   E. Acted like Joe in the store
___ 6. JODY   F. Narrator of the story
___ 7. NUNKIE   G. Vergible _____; Tea Cake
___ 8. NANNY   H. Joe's nickname
___ 9. DOG   I. Town celebrated its installation; street ___
___ 10. LAMP   J. Made a play for Tea Cake
___ 11. JACKSONVILLE   K. Tea Cake's weapon
___ 12. COODEMAY   L. Tea Cake's first symptom
___ 13. TRIAL   M. Tea Cake tried to put him out of the restaurant
___ 14. BOOTYNY   N. First to hear Janie's story
___ 15. SOP   O. Threw his coffee cup at Coodemay
___ 16. PHOEBY   P. Wanted to testify at Janie's trial: ___-de-Bottom
___ 17. WOODS   Q. Disease Tea Cake got from dog
___ 18. OKECHOBEE   R. Overflowing lake
___ 19. RABIES   S. Site of Tea Cake and Janie's wedding
___ 20. PISTOL   T. Held the same day as Tea Cake's death
___ 21. HEADACHE   U. Tea Cake killed it to save Janie
___ 22. TURNER   V. Slept through the hurricane
___ 23. KILLICKS   W. Joe made Janie wear them in the store
___ 24. HEZEKIAH   X. Tea ____
___ 25. JANIE   Y. Last name of Janie's farmer husband

Their Eyes Were Watching God Matching 2 Answer Key

A - 1. GAMBLING	A.	How Tea Cake got Janie's money back
B - 2. RIFLE	B.	Janie's weapon
W - 3. HEADRAGS	C.	Raised Janie
V - 4. MOTORBOAT	D.	Mrs. ___ didn't like dark-skinned Blacks
X - 5. CAKE	E.	Acted like Joe in the store
H - 6. JODY	F.	Narrator of the story
J - 7. NUNKIE	G.	Vergible _____; Tea Cake
C - 8. NANNY	H.	Joe's nickname
U - 9. DOG	I.	Town celebrated its installation; street ___
I - 10. LAMP	J.	Made a play for Tea Cake
S - 11. JACKSONVILLE	K.	Tea Cake's weapon
M - 12. COODEMAY	L.	Tea Cake's first symptom
T - 13. TRIAL	M.	Tea Cake tried to put him out of the restaurant
O - 14. BOOTYNY	N.	First to hear Janie's story
P - 15. SOP	O.	Threw his coffee cup at Coodemay
N - 16. PHOEBY	P.	Wanted to testify at Janie's trial: ___-de-Bottom
G - 17. WOODS	Q.	Disease Tea Cake got from dog
R - 18. OKECHOBEE	R.	Overflowing lake
Q - 19. RABIES	S.	Site of Tea Cake and Janie's wedding
K - 20. PISTOL	T.	Held the same day as Tea Cake's death
L - 21. HEADACHE	U.	Tea Cake killed it to save Janie
D - 22. TURNER	V.	Slept through the hurricane
Y - 23. KILLICKS	W.	Joe made Janie wear them in the store
E - 24. HEZEKIAH	X.	Tea ____
F - 25. JANIE	Y.	Last name of Janie's farmer husband

Their Eyes Were Watching God Matching 3

___ 1. EATONVILLE   A. Joe's nickname
___ 2. MULE   B. Nanny compared the black woman to one
___ 3. SOP   C. Made a play for Tea Cake
___ 4. TRIAL   D. Tea Cake tried to put him out of the restaurant
___ 5. MOURNING   E. Joe started one in Eatonville
___ 6. OKECHOBEE   F. Narrator of the story
___ 7. RABIES   G. Tea ____
___ 8. KILLICKS   H. Janie's weapon
___ 9. COODEMAY   I. Janie's most noticeable physical characteristic
___10. NANNY   J. Raised Janie
___11. NUNKIE   K. Town where Joe and Janie settled
___12. MAYOR   L. Held the same day as Tea Cake's death
___13. CAKE   M. Slept through the hurricane
___14. SERRENT   N. Last name of Janie's farmer husband
___15. STORE   O. Joe was the first one in Eatonville
___16. RIFLE   P. Crop they picked on the muck
___17. JANIE   Q. Tea Cake's weapon
___18. PISTOL   R. Disease Tea Cake got from dog
___19. BEANS   S. Mr. Killicks' first name
___20. HEADRAGS   T. Drunken instigator of fight at the restaurant
___21. JODY   U. It shouldn't last any longer than grief
___22. SEMINOLES   V. Janie watched a band of them leave the muck
___23. LOGAN   W. Wanted to testify at Janie's trial: ____-de-Bottom
___24. HAIR   X. Joe made Janie wear them in the store
___25. MOTORBOAT   Y. Overflowing lake

Their Eyes Were Watching God Matching 3 Answer Key

K - 1. EATONVILLE	A.	Joe's nickname
B - 2. MULE	B.	Nanny compared the black woman to one
W - 3. SOP	C.	Made a play for Tea Cake
L - 4. TRIAL	D.	Tea Cake tried to put him out of the restaurant
U - 5. MOURNING	E.	Joe started one in Eatonville
Y - 6. OKECHOBEE	F.	Narrator of the story
R - 7. RABIES	G.	Tea ____
N - 8. KILLICKS	H.	Janie's weapon
D - 9. COODEMAY	I.	Janie's most noticeable physical characteristic
J - 10. NANNY	J.	Raised Janie
C - 11. NUNKIE	K.	Town where Joe and Janie settled
O - 12. MAYOR	L.	Held the same day as Tea Cake's death
G - 13. CAKE	M.	Slept through the hurricane
T - 14. SERRENT	N.	Last name of Janie's farmer husband
E - 15. STORE	O.	Joe was the first one in Eatonville
H - 16. RIFLE	P.	Crop they picked on the muck
F - 17. JANIE	Q.	Tea Cake's weapon
Q - 18. PISTOL	R.	Disease Tea Cake got from dog
P - 19. BEANS	S.	Mr. Killicks' first name
X - 20. HEADRAGS	T.	Drunken instigator of fight at the restaurant
A - 21. JODY	U.	It shouldn't last any longer than grief
V - 22. SEMINOLES	V.	Janie watched a band of them leave the muck
S - 23. LOGAN	W.	Wanted to testify at Janie's trial: ____-de-Bottom
I - 24. HAIR	X.	Joe made Janie wear them in the store
M - 25. MOTORBOAT	Y.	Overflowing lake

Their Eyes Were Watching God Matching 4

___ 1. DOG   A. Tea Cake's first symptom
___ 2. LAMP   B. Town where Joe and Janie settled
___ 3. CAKE   C. Raised Janie
___ 4. RABIES   D. Doctor who testified in Janie's behalf
___ 5. MAYOR   E. Tea Cake killed it to save Janie
___ 6. LOGAN   F. Acted like Joe in the store
___ 7. SOP   G. Joe's nickname
___ 8. EATONVILLE   H. Town celebrated its installation; street ___
___ 9. EVERGLADES   I. Disease Tea Cake got from dog
___10. NANNY   J. Tea ____
___11. RIFLE   K. What Tea Cake called the Everglade crop land
___12. STORE   L. Vergible _____; Tea Cake
___13. HEZEKIAH   M. Joe started one in Eatonville
___14. MOURNING   N. Janie watched a band of them leave the muck
___15. HAIR   O. Joe was the first one in Eatonville
___16. NUNKIE   P. Tea Cake tried to put him out of the restaurant
___17. JODY   Q. Location of the muck
___18. SERRENT   R. Slept through the hurricane
___19. SIMMONS   S. Made a play for Tea Cake
___20. COODEMAY   T. Wanted to testify at Janie's trial: ___-de-Bottom
___21. MUCK   U. Mr. Killicks' first name
___22. MOTORBOAT   V. Drunken instigator of fight at the restaurant
___23. WOODS   W. Janie's most noticeable physical characteristic
___24. SEMINOLES   X. It shouldn't last any longer than grief
___25. HEADACHE   Y. Janie's weapon

Their Eyes Were Watching God Matching 4 Answer Key

E - 1.	DOG	A. Tea Cake's first symptom
H - 2.	LAMP	B. Town where Joe and Janie settled
J - 3.	CAKE	C. Raised Janie
I - 4.	RABIES	D. Doctor who testified in Janie's behalf
O - 5.	MAYOR	E. Tea Cake killed it to save Janie
U - 6.	LOGAN	F. Acted like Joe in the store
T - 7.	SOP	G. Joe's nickname
B - 8.	EATONVILLE	H. Town celebrated its installation; street ___
Q - 9.	EVERGLADES	I. Disease Tea Cake got from dog
C - 10.	NANNY	J. Tea ____
Y - 11.	RIFLE	K. What Tea Cake called the Everglade crop land
M - 12.	STORE	L. Vergible _____; Tea Cake
F - 13.	HEZEKIAH	M. Joe started one in Eatonville
X - 14.	MOURNING	N. Janie watched a band of them leave the muck
W - 15.	HAIR	O. Joe was the first one in Eatonville
S - 16.	NUNKIE	P. Tea Cake tried to put him out of the restaurant
G - 17.	JODY	Q. Location of the muck
V - 18.	SERRENT	R. Slept through the hurricane
D - 19.	SIMMONS	S. Made a play for Tea Cake
P - 20.	COODEMAY	T. Wanted to testify at Janie's trial: ___-de-Bottom
K - 21.	MUCK	U. Mr. Killicks' first name
R - 22.	MOTORBOAT	V. Drunken instigator of fight at the restaurant
L - 23.	WOODS	W. Janie's most noticeable physical characteristic
N - 24.	SEMINOLES	X. It shouldn't last any longer than grief
A - 25.	HEADACHE	Y. Janie's weapon

Their Eyes Were Watching God Matching 1

Match the definition with the vocabulary word. Put your answers in the magic squares below. When your answers are correct, all columns and rows will add to the same number.

A. EATONVILLE
B. SIMMONS
C. MAYOR
D. SEEDS
E. DOG
F. SOP
G. EVERGLADES
H. BEANS
I. KILLICKS
J. WOODS
K. HAIR
L. PISTOL
M. GAMBLING
N. LAMP
O. HEZEKIAH
P. HURRICANE

1. Crop they picked on the muck
2. How Tea Cake got Janie's money back
3. Doctor who testified in Janie's behalf
4. Janie's most noticeable physical characteristic
5. Vergible _____; Tea Cake
6. Joe was the first one in Eatonville
7. Caused evacuation of the muck
8. Tea Cake killed it to save Janie
9. Acted like Joe in the store
10. Wanted to testify at Janie's trial: ___-de-Bottom
11. Last name of Janie's farmer husband
12. Janie brought these back from the muck
13. Town where Joe and Janie settled
14. Tea Cake's weapon
15. Location of the muck
16. Town celebrated its installation; street ___

A=	B=	C=	D=
E=	F=	G=	H=
I=	J=	K=	L=
M=	N=	O=	P=

Their Eyes Were Watching God Matching 1 Answer Key

Match the definition with the vocabulary word. Put your answers in the magic squares below. When your answers are correct, all columns and rows will add to the same number.

A. EATONVILLE
B. SIMMONS
C. MAYOR
D. SEEDS
E. DOG
F. SOP
G. EVERGLADES
H. BEANS
I. KILLICKS
J. WOODS
K. HAIR
L. PISTOL
M. GAMBLING
N. LAMP
O. HEZEKIAH
P. HURRICANE

1. Crop they picked on the muck
2. How Tea Cake got Janie's money back
3. Doctor who testified in Janie's behalf
4. Janie's most noticeable physical characteristic
5. Vergible _____; Tea Cake
6. Joe was the first one in Eatonville
7. Caused evacuation of the muck
8. Tea Cake killed it to save Janie
9. Acted like Joe in the store
10. Wanted to testify at Janie's trial: ___-de-Bottom
11. Last name of Janie's farmer husband
12. Janie brought these back from the muck
13. Town where Joe and Janie settled
14. Tea Cake's weapon
15. Location of the muck
16. Town celebrated its installation; street ___

A=13	B=3	C=6	D=12
E=8	F=10	G=15	H=1
I=11	J=5	K=4	L=14
M=2	N=16	O=9	P=7

Their Eyes Were Watching God Matching 2

Match the definition with the vocabulary word. Put your answers in the magic squares below. When your answers are correct, all columns and rows will add to the same number.

A. CAKE
B. RABIES
C. BEANS
D. MULE
E. JACKSONVILLE
F. SERRENT
G. SWALLOW
H. PHOEBY
I. HEADRAGS
J. DOG
K. HURRICANE
L. HAIR
M. OKECHOBEE
N. RIFLE
O. SEMINOLES
P. JANIE

1. Tea ____
2. Janie's weapon
3. Tea Cake killed it to save Janie
4. Site of Tea Cake and Janie's wedding
5. What Tea Cake couldn't do when he was sick
6. Janie's most noticeable physical characteristic
7. Narrator of the story
8. Crop they picked on the muck
9. Janie watched a band of them leave the muck
10. Nanny compared the black woman to one
11. First to hear Janie's story
12. Caused evacuation of the muck
13. Joe made Janie wear them in the store
14. Drunken instigator of fight at the restaurant
15. Disease Tea Cake got from dog
16. Overflowing lake

A=	B=	C=	D=
E=	F=	G=	H=
I=	J=	K=	L=
M=	N=	O=	P=

Their Eyes Were Watching God Matching 2 Answer Key

Match the definition with the vocabulary word. Put your answers in the magic squares below. When your answers are correct, all columns and rows will add to the same number.

A. CAKE
B. RABIES
C. BEANS
D. MULE
E. JACKSONVILLE
F. SERRENT
G. SWALLOW
H. PHOEBY
I. HEADRAGS
J. DOG
K. HURRICANE
L. HAIR
M. OKECHOBEE
N. RIFLE
O. SEMINOLES
P. JANIE

1. Tea ____
2. Janie's weapon
3. Tea Cake killed it to save Janie
4. Site of Tea Cake and Janie's wedding
5. What Tea Cake couldn't do when he was sick
6. Janie's most noticeable physical characteristic
7. Narrator of the story
8. Crop they picked on the muck
9. Janie watched a band of them leave the muck
10. Nanny compared the black woman to one
11. First to hear Janie's story
12. Caused evacuation of the muck
13. Joe made Janie wear them in the store
14. Drunken instigator of fight at the restaurant
15. Disease Tea Cake got from dog
16. Overflowing lake

A=1	B=15	C=8	D=10
E=4	F=14	G=5	H=11
I=13	J=3	K=12	L=6
M=16	N=2	O=9	P=7

Their Eyes Were Watching God Matching 3

Match the definition with the vocabulary word. Put your answers in the magic squares below. When your answers are correct, all columns and rows will add to the same number.

A. GAMBLING
B. JOE
C. HEADRAGS
D. STORE
E. SIMMONS
F. BEANS
G. EATONVILLE
H. SWALLOW
I. MUCK
J. DOG
K. HURRICANE
L. JODY
M. MOTORBOAT
N. LAMP
O. HEADACHE
P. PISTOL

1. Town celebrated its installation; street ___
2. Town where Joe and Janie settled
3. Joe's nickname
4. How Tea Cake got Janie's money back
5. Caused evacuation of the muck
6. Janie's businessman-mayor husband
7. Slept through the hurricane
8. What Tea Cake couldn't do when he was sick
9. Doctor who testified in Janie's behalf
10. Tea Cake's weapon
11. Joe made Janie wear them in the store
12. Tea Cake killed it to save Janie
13. Joe started one in Eatonville
14. What Tea Cake called the Everglade crop land
15. Crop they picked on the muck
16. Tea Cake's first symptom

A=	B=	C=	D=
E=	F=	G=	H=
I=	J=	K=	L=
M=	N=	O=	P=

Their Eyes Were Watching God Matching 3 Answer Key

Match the definition with the vocabulary word. Put your answers in the magic squares below. When your answers are correct, all columns and rows will add to the same number.

A. GAMBLING
B. JOE
C. HEADRAGS
D. STORE
E. SIMMONS
F. BEANS
G. EATONVILLE
H. SWALLOW
I. MUCK
J. DOG
K. HURRICANE
L. JODY
M. MOTORBOAT
N. LAMP
O. HEADACHE
P. PISTOL

1. Town celebrated its installation; street ___
2. Town where Joe and Janie settled
3. Joe's nickname
4. How Tea Cake got Janie's money back
5. Caused evacuation of the muck
6. Janie's businessman-mayor husband
7. Slept through the hurricane
8. What Tea Cake couldn't do when he was sick
9. Doctor who testified in Janie's behalf
10. Tea Cake's weapon
11. Joe made Janie wear them in the store
12. Tea Cake killed it to save Janie
13. Joe started one in Eatonville
14. What Tea Cake called the Everglade crop land
15. Crop they picked on the muck
16. Tea Cake's first symptom

A=4	B=6	C=11	D=13
E=9	F=15	G=2	H=8
I=14	J=12	K=5	L=3
M=7	N=1	O=16	P=10

Their Eyes Were Watching God Matching 4

Match the definition with the vocabulary word. Put your answers in the magic squares below. When your answers are correct, all columns and rows will add to the same number.

A. SEEDS
B. JODY
C. TURNER
D. CAKE
E. HURRICANE
F. SIMMONS
G. JACKSONVILLE
H. PISTOL
I. MOTORBOAT
J. NUNKIE
K. KILLICKS
L. STORE
M. RABIES
N. DOG
O. HEADACHE
P. WOODS

1. Tea Cake's first symptom
2. Tea ____
3. Made a play for Tea Cake
4. Caused evacuation of the muck
5. Slept through the hurricane
6. Doctor who testified in Janie's behalf
7. Vergible _____; Tea Cake
8. Mrs. ___ didn't like dark-skinned Blacks
9. Tea Cake's weapon
10. Last name of Janie's farmer husband
11. Janie brought these back from the muck
12. Tea Cake killed it to save Janie
13. Joe's nickname
14. Disease Tea Cake got from dog
15. Site of Tea Cake and Janie's wedding
16. Joe started one in Eatonville

A=	B=	C=	D=
E=	F=	G=	H=
I=	J=	K=	L=
M=	N=	O=	P=

Their Eyes Were Watching God Matching 4 Answer Key

Match the definition with the vocabulary word. Put your answers in the magic squares below. When your answers are correct, all columns and rows will add to the same number.

A. SEEDS
B. JODY
C. TURNER
D. CAKE
E. HURRICANE
F. SIMMONS
G. JACKSONVILLE
H. PISTOL
I. MOTORBOAT
J. NUNKIE
K. KILLICKS
L. STORE
M. RABIES
N. DOG
O. HEADACHE
P. WOODS

1. Tea Cake's first symptom
2. Tea ____
3. Made a play for Tea Cake
4. Caused evacuation of the muck
5. Slept through the hurricane
6. Doctor who testified in Janie's behalf
7. Vergible ____; Tea Cake
8. Mrs. ___ didn't like dark-skinned Blacks
9. Tea Cake's weapon
10. Last name of Janie's farmer husband
11. Janie brought these back from the muck
12. Tea Cake killed it to save Janie
13. Joe's nickname
14. Disease Tea Cake got from dog
15. Site of Tea Cake and Janie's wedding
16. Joe started one in Eatonville

A=11	B=13	C=8	D=2
E=4	F=6	G=15	H=9
I=5	J=3	K=10	L=16
M=14	N=12	O=1	P=7

Their Eyes Were Watching God Word Search 1

Words are placed backwards, forward, diagonally, up and down. Clues listed below can help you find the words. Circle the hidden vocabulary words in the maze.

```
S G A R D A E H C A D A E H N A N N Y B
I E D W F V E Z M N F G I M A N M S J W
M K E D P N B H S C B R K K S I E H O P
M V T D S J O S U Q R Y N F W D R D D Z
O X Q R S B H E G R K C U M A Q E B Y T
N Z T I Q L C M V S R J N L L L L B H J
S B G F D L E I C E W I G H L V L F E J
G E S L X L K N R H H R C I O S I D Z T
B A T E O K O O X M E K V A W C V X E Q
X N M T X W T L X V P N I V N T N V K D
T S S B M S M E E C O W X L P E O N I H
Z I P H L Q S S V T Y O K K L K S Z A M
P N C V T I X G A Q Q O S N P I K M H H
M B K Y L Q N E Z M P D H P B V C G Z J
G S L W G G B G F Y T S P P M V A K K K
T X M H K N N B R F X N T L B T J R S X
C N H O X Y V N B M S F A Z T V J Q N S
P R N P U L K Y O X F T O N K N P P B Z
K J X T H R L N O Y N T B R D M V T K S
M N Y U T O N W T M M S R F C N E V S G
N U H R M J E I Y D A K O G A V I T P B
H Q L N T D C B N O R Y T G K Y N M J Z
P O S E I B A R Y G C O O D E M A Y O T
S E R R E N T T R I A L M R Z L J J E K
```

Acted like Joe in the store (8)
Caused evacuation of the muck (9)
Crop they picked on the muck (5)
Disease Tea Cake got from dog (6)
Doctor who testified in Janie's behalf (7)
Drunken instigator of fight at the restaurant (7)
First to hear Janie's story (6)
Held the same day as Tea Cake's death (5)
How Tea Cake got Janie's money back (8)
It shouldn't last any longer than grief (8)
Janie brought these back from the muck (5)
Janie watched a band of them leave the muck (9)
Janie's businessman-mayor husband (3)
Janie's most noticeable physical characteristic (4)
Janie's weapon (5)
Joe made Janie wear them in the store (8)
Joe started one in Eatonville (5)
Joe was the first one in Eatonville (5)
Joe's nickname (4)
Last name of Janie's farmer husband (8)
Location of the muck (10)
Made a play for Tea Cake (6)
Mr. Killicks' first name (5)

Mrs. ___ didn't like dark-skinned Blacks (6)
Nanny compared the black woman to one (4)
Narrator of the story (5)
Overflowing lake (9)
Raised Janie (5)
Site of Tea Cake and Janie's wedding (12)
Slept through the hurricane (9)
Tea Cake killed it to save Janie (3)
Tea Cake tried to put him out of the restaurant (8)
Tea Cake's first symptom (8)
Tea Cake's weapon (6)
Tea ____ (4)
Threw his coffee cup at Coodemay (7)
Town celebrated its installation; street ___ (4)
Town where Joe and Janie settled (10)
Vergible _____; Tea Cake (5)
Wanted to testify at Janie's trial: ___-de-Bottom (3)
What Tea Cake called the Everglade crop land (4)
What Tea Cake couldn't do when he was sick (7)

Their Eyes Were Watching God Word Search 1 Answer Key

Words are placed backwards, forward, diagonally, up and down. Clues listed below can help you find the words. Circle the hidden vocabulary words in the maze.

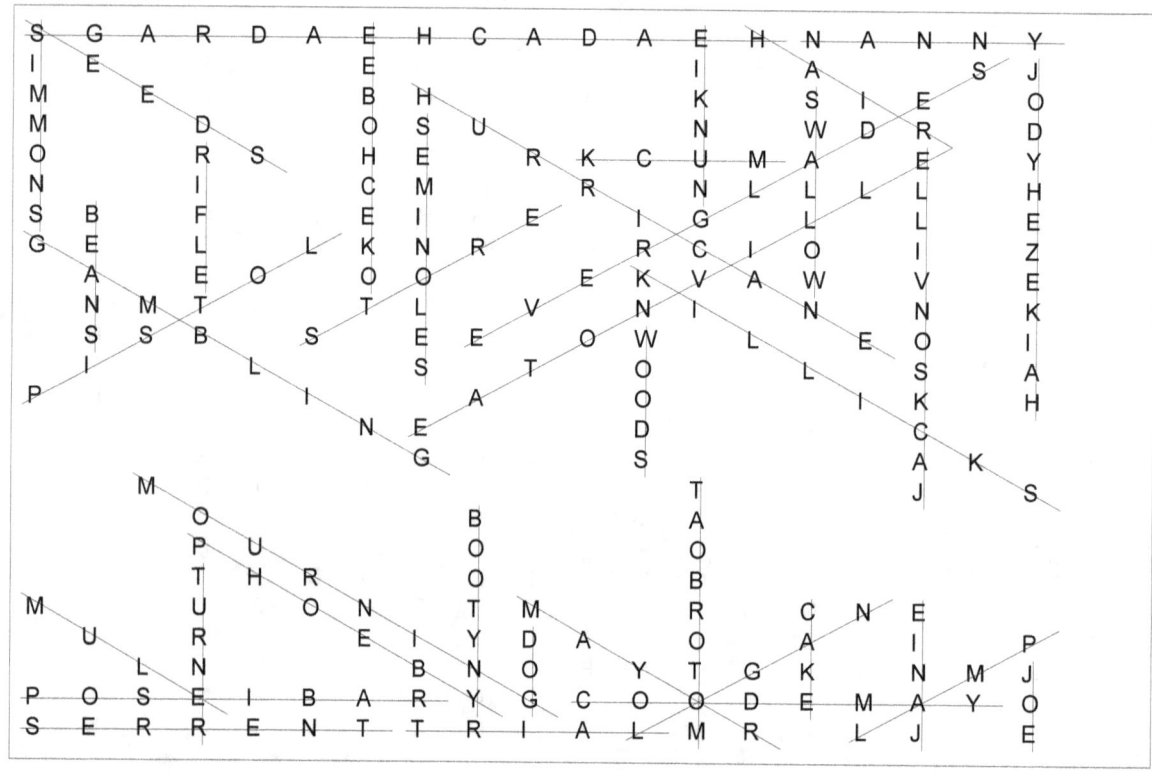

Acted like Joe in the store (8)
Caused evacuation of the muck (9)
Crop they picked on the muck (5)
Disease Tea Cake got from dog (6)
Doctor who testified in Janie's behalf (7)
Drunken instigator of fight at the restaurant (7)
First to hear Janie's story (6)
Held the same day as Tea Cake's death (5)
How Tea Cake got Janie's money back (8)
It shouldn't last any longer than grief (8)
Janie brought these back from the muck (5)
Janie watched a band of them leave the muck (9)
Janie's businessman-mayor husband (3)
Janie's most noticeable physical characteristic (4)
Janie's weapon (5)
Joe made Janie wear them in the store (8)
Joe started one in Eatonville (5)
Joe was the first one in Eatonville (5)
Joe's nickname (4)
Last name of Janie's farmer husband (8)
Location of the muck (10)
Made a play for Tea Cake (6)
Mr. Killicks' first name (5)

Mrs. ___ didn't like dark-skinned Blacks (6)
Nanny compared the black woman to one (4)
Narrator of the story (5)
Overflowing lake (9)
Raised Janie (5)
Site of Tea Cake and Janie's wedding (12)
Slept through the hurricane (9)
Tea Cake killed it to save Janie (3)
Tea Cake tried to put him out of the restaurant (8)
Tea Cake's first symptom (8)
Tea Cake's weapon (6)
Tea ____ (4)
Threw his coffee cup at Coodemay (7)
Town celebrated its installation; street ___ (4)
Town where Joe and Janie settled (10)
Vergible _____; Tea Cake (5)
Wanted to testify at Janie's trial: ___-de-Bottom (3)
What Tea Cake called the Everglade crop land (4)
What Tea Cake couldn't do when he was sick (7)

Their Eyes Were Watching God Word Search 2

Words are placed backwards, forward, diagonally, up and down. Clues listed below can help you find the words. Circle the hidden vocabulary words in the maze.

```
B T R I A L E J P I S T O L G O D T M L
H E J Z T L S A O W C H N N A G A F A W
P E A J Z Z R E T D K N T S M O K M Y M
C I A N J S X G E O Y T N W B M M O O Q
B K J D S E M R J D N F Z R L U L U R G
W N C W R D G T R Z S V O J I C Y R L L
Z U L D K A C X P K Y T I H N K V N R E
Y N N A N L G O J M O C E L G S E I K S
V Z X Z G G K S O M X N M V L H H N I T
Q P R V K R N T T D A L Y H C E N G L Q
B C Y D C E R M V C E P Y A V F R E L L
L D Y W S V P K I Q D M D S V R M L I W
K Z C R L E S R L L M A A J T Y M L C G
P R N V S L R W T J E D K Y J X S I K S
S J V P M U C H L H Y Q S V T B L V S X
S G F F H X D E N D O Y E F M R Y N R D
W W V G W B P Z F G K X M R F N V O T Q
A T D W N R W E S N E W I J Y P S S L K
L F U D G I X K I C C T N T M Z E K O H
L S W R M F L I M A H R O N V M I C G X
O T S N N L S A M K O O L T C R B A A M
W O O D S E P H O E B Y E E I N A J N J
M R Z T X G R H N Y E R S A M R R Z O R
C E L A M P O S S B E Z H S E R R E N T
```

Acted like Joe in the store (8)
Caused evacuation of the muck (9)
Crop they picked on the muck (5)
Disease Tea Cake got from dog (6)
Doctor who testified in Janie's behalf (7)
Drunken instigator of fight at the restaurant (7)
First to hear Janie's story (6)
Held the same day as Tea Cake's death (5)
How Tea Cake got Janie's money back (8)
It shouldn't last any longer than grief (8)
Janie brought these back from the muck (5)
Janie watched a band of them leave the muck (9)
Janie's businessman-mayor husband (3)
Janie's most noticeable physical characteristic (4)
Janie's weapon (5)
Joe made Janie wear them in the store (8)
Joe started one in Eatonville (5)
Joe was the first one in Eatonville (5)
Joe's nickname (4)
Last name of Janie's farmer husband (8)
Location of the muck (10)
Made a play for Tea Cake (6)
Mr. Killicks' first name (5)

Mrs. ___ didn't like dark-skinned Blacks (6)
Nanny compared the black woman to one (4)
Narrator of the story (5)
Overflowing lake (9)
Raised Janie (5)
Site of Tea Cake and Janie's wedding (12)
Slept through the hurricane (9)
Tea Cake killed it to save Janie (3)
Tea Cake tried to put him out of the restaurant (8)
Tea Cake's first symptom (8)
Tea Cake's weapon (6)
Tea ____ (4)
Threw his coffee cup at Coodemay (7)
Town celebrated its installation; street ___ (4)
Town where Joe and Janie settled (10)
Vergible _____; Tea Cake (5)
Wanted to testify at Janie's trial: ___-de-Bottom (3)
What Tea Cake called the Everglade crop land (4)
What Tea Cake couldn't do when he was sick (7)

Their Eyes Were Watching God Word Search 2 Answer Key

Words are placed backwards, forward, diagonally, up and down. Clues listed below can help you find the words. Circle the hidden vocabulary words in the maze.

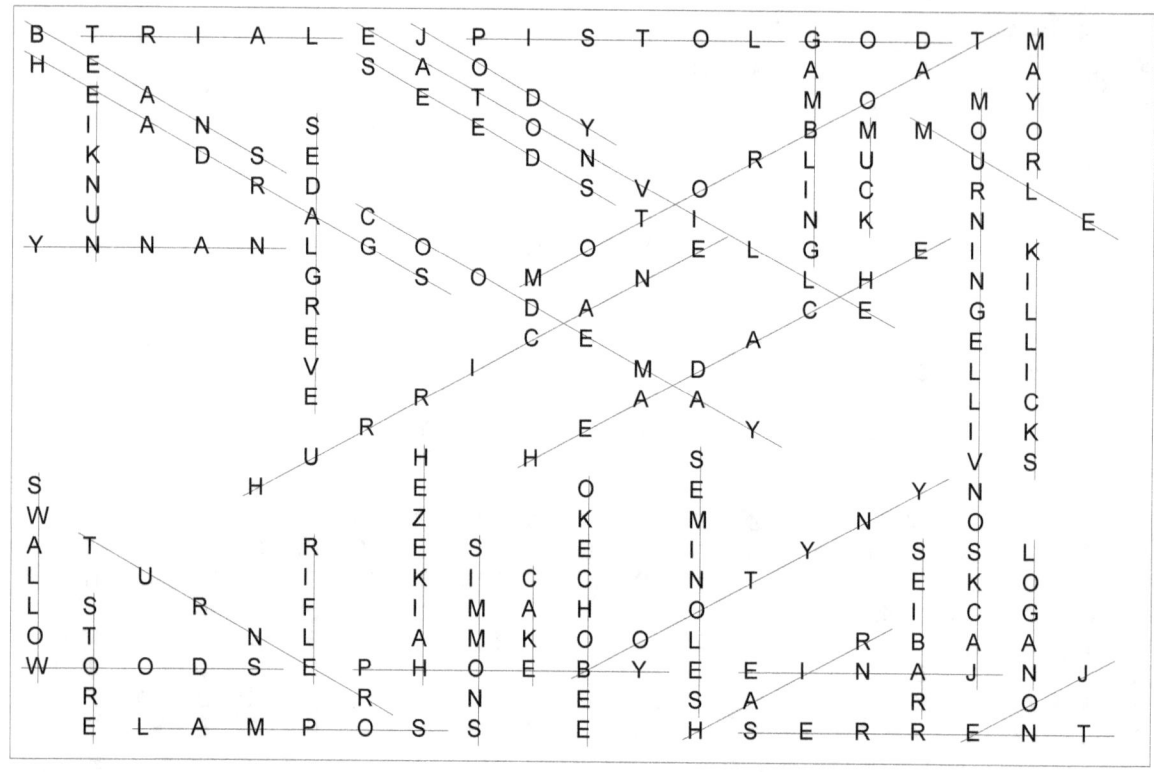

Acted like Joe in the store (8)
Caused evacuation of the muck (9)
Crop they picked on the muck (5)
Disease Tea Cake got from dog (6)
Doctor who testified in Janie's behalf (7)
Drunken instigator of fight at the restaurant (7)
First to hear Janie's story (6)
Held the same day as Tea Cake's death (5)
How Tea Cake got Janie's money back (8)
It shouldn't last any longer than grief (8)
Janie brought these back from the muck (5)
Janie watched a band of them leave the muck (9)
Janie's businessman-mayor husband (3)
Janie's most noticeable physical characteristic (4)
Janie's weapon (5)
Joe made Janie wear them in the store (8)
Joe started one in Eatonville (5)
Joe was the first one in Eatonville (5)
Joe's nickname (4)
Last name of Janie's farmer husband (8)
Location of the muck (10)
Made a play for Tea Cake (6)
Mr. Killicks' first name (5)

Mrs. ___ didn't like dark-skinned Blacks (6)
Nanny compared the black woman to one (4)
Narrator of the story (5)
Overflowing lake (9)
Raised Janie (5)
Site of Tea Cake and Janie's wedding (12)
Slept through the hurricane (9)
Tea Cake killed it to save Janie (3)
Tea Cake tried to put him out of the restaurant (8)
Tea Cake's first symptom (8)
Tea Cake's weapon (6)
Tea ____ (4)
Threw his coffee cup at Coodemay (7)
Town celebrated its installation; street ___ (4)
Town where Joe and Janie settled (10)
Vergible _____; Tea Cake (5)
Wanted to testify at Janie's trial: ___-de-Bottom (3)
What Tea Cake called the Everglade crop land (4)
What Tea Cake couldn't do when he was sick (7)

Their Eyes Were Watching God Word Search 3

Words are placed backwards, forward, diagonally, up and down. Words listed below are included in the maze. Circle the hidden vocabulary words in the maze.

```
P Q N K B O O T Y N Y A M E D O O C E Q
Q T L R C S S M O T O R B O A T W E K S
T Z K G L P V H Y S Z F K E N L B H X G
E V E R G L A D E S L H S J A O Z Y P H
Y H M S P I K Q L E D Q O T H N V J N S
J P F H K R J Y N L A M P C R C S N T V
P D G E R T T A J X Q Q E M T D W E R F
J D Z G E R C Y O D G K V X O C A L I Q
P E D C N I J L D P O M P O G A L U A N
H E A D R A G S Y I M G W C H K L M L B
V L T R U H B N V S K K F C I E O V O G
B G U B T R N W F T N Z X L S U W S G Y
T H S V N A H R K O V R L N R K N N A J
T M M D N J E W N L N I X N J O E C N G
M Y N U A Y A A L J C U I Q M N N D F C
Y H B N C F D D T K S N N M H N C X F R
S V I F F K A P S O G Y I K K X G S M Q
S E L F I R C M H R N S E M I N O L E S
T Y R V H M H A B O H V Y M I E C B G R
O T P R J D E Y V V E G I L Q L R B A F
R B C S E T S O Y F K B B L S Z L B W S
E P B L V N W R Y G B M Y L L Z I F D V
L M R T T N T J B S A R F K G E P V K T
T N J P S L T F W G S E E D S L H K S C
```

BEANS	HEADACHE	LOGAN	PHOEBY	STORE
BOOTYNY	HEADRAGS	MAYOR	PISTOL	SWALLOW
CAKE	HEZEKIAH	MOTORBOAT	RABIES	TRIAL
COODEMAY	HURRICANE	MOURNING	RIFLE	TURNER
DOG	JANIE	MUCK	SEEDS	WOODS
EATONVILLE	JODY	MULE	SEMINOLES	
EVERGLADES	JOE	NANNY	SERRENT	
GAMBLING	KILLICKS	NUNKIE	SIMMONS	
HAIR	LAMP	OKECHOBEE	SOP	

Their Eyes Were Watching God Word Search 3 Answer Key

Words are placed backwards, forward, diagonally, up and down. Words listed below are included in the maze. Circle the hidden vocabulary words in the maze.

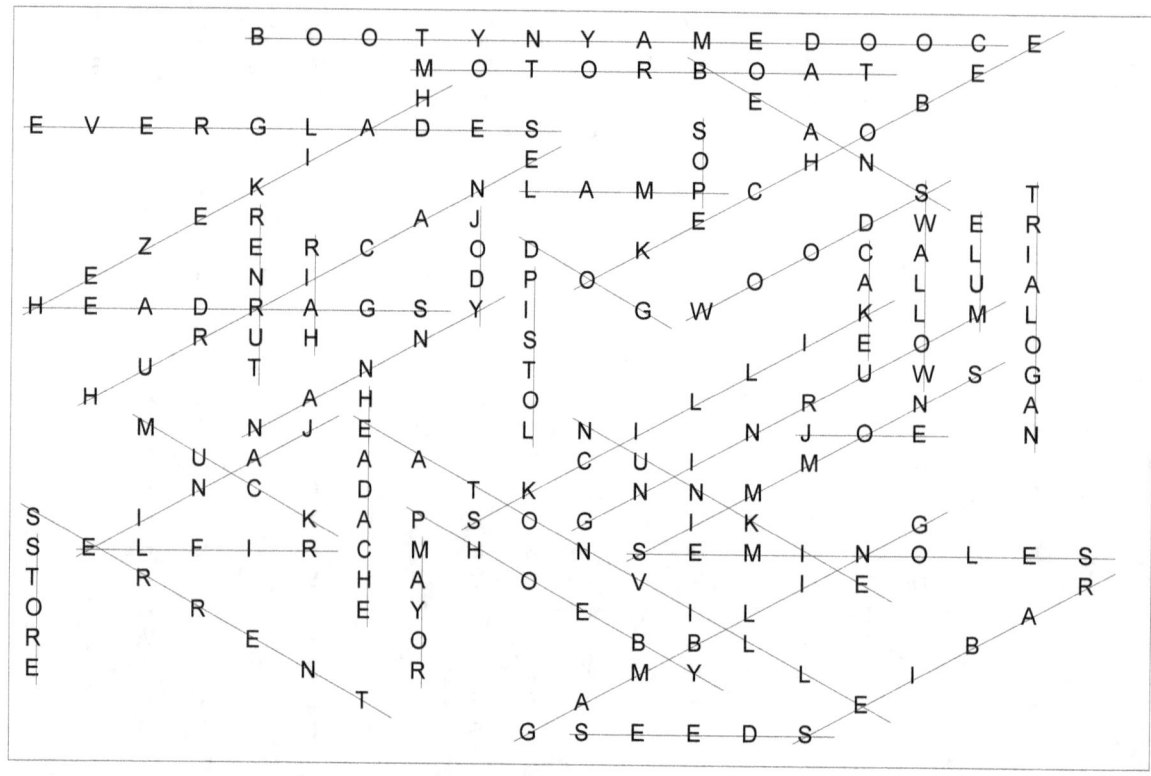

BEANS	HEADACHE	LOGAN	PHOEBY	STORE
BOOTYNY	HEADRAGS	MAYOR	PISTOL	SWALLOW
CAKE	HEZEKIAH	MOTORBOAT	RABIES	TRIAL
COODEMAY	HURRICANE	MOURNING	RIFLE	TURNER
DOG	JANIE	MUCK	SEEDS	WOODS
EATONVILLE	JODY	MULE	SEMINOLES	
EVERGLADES	JOE	NANNY	SERRENT	
GAMBLING	KILLICKS	NUNKIE	SIMMONS	
HAIR	LAMP	OKECHOBEE	SOP	

Their Eyes Were Watching God Word Search 4

Words are placed backwards, forward, diagonally, up and down. Words listed below are included in the maze. Circle the hidden vocabulary words in the maze.

```
Q M N M H S F S K J R T H P N S G M S N
B M A Y O R E D O G I M U L E W J O D Y
G T G N B I O R N T F V R A K A P T O Y
G F O N B L J I R W L K R I A L G O O C
B F L A C C N K M E E R I R C L A R W M
H W R C P R S I N N N K C T X O M B G N
F E C F U B E L S V M T A S C W B O J T
J J A O Z Y E L S Q D K N Y V P L A J S
S A M D G K D I S E D O E R G F I T T S
V J N F R V S C Y A M E D O O C N L U W
Z F S I X A V K M M Z I Z Z S Z G A R X
N O J K E P G S I P P H N K G J N M N G
N Y K P Q D P S J R G T C O M V S P E G
H E Z E K I A H W F S U G B L S T O R E
B V S M C Z X S O E M S H O O E P T M S
E D F N P H V P D E M B T E Z O S B S C
A C V F Z M O A X G B S N P A D T R J P
N Y N L V B L B R W I Y U K M D I Y F T
S H D P C G S Z E P T V N L L A A M N D
M K Q F R L P X C E K M K X H J L C V Y
Z Y D E K M Q P N Y H Q I K H J L Z H T
H K V W Y S F F S J Z G E C B H W K N E
K E A T O N V I L L E W N R T F B K W
J A C K S O N V I L L E N D N S M D N P
```

BEANS	HEADACHE	LAMP	OKECHOBEE	SOP
BOOTYNY	HEADRAGS	LOGAN	PHOEBY	STORE
CAKE	HEZEKIAH	MAYOR	PISTOL	SWALLOW
COODEMAY	HURRICANE	MOTORBOAT	RABIES	TRIAL
DOG	JACKSONVILLE	MOURNING	RIFLE	TURNER
EATONVILLE	JANIE	MUCK	SEEDS	WOODS
EVERGLADES	JODY	MULE	SEMINOLES	
GAMBLING	JOE	NANNY	SERRENT	
HAIR	KILLICKS	NUNKIE	SIMMONS	

Their Eyes Were Watching God Word Search 4 Answer Key

Words are placed backwards, forward, diagonally, up and down. Words listed below are included in the maze. Circle the hidden vocabulary words in the maze.

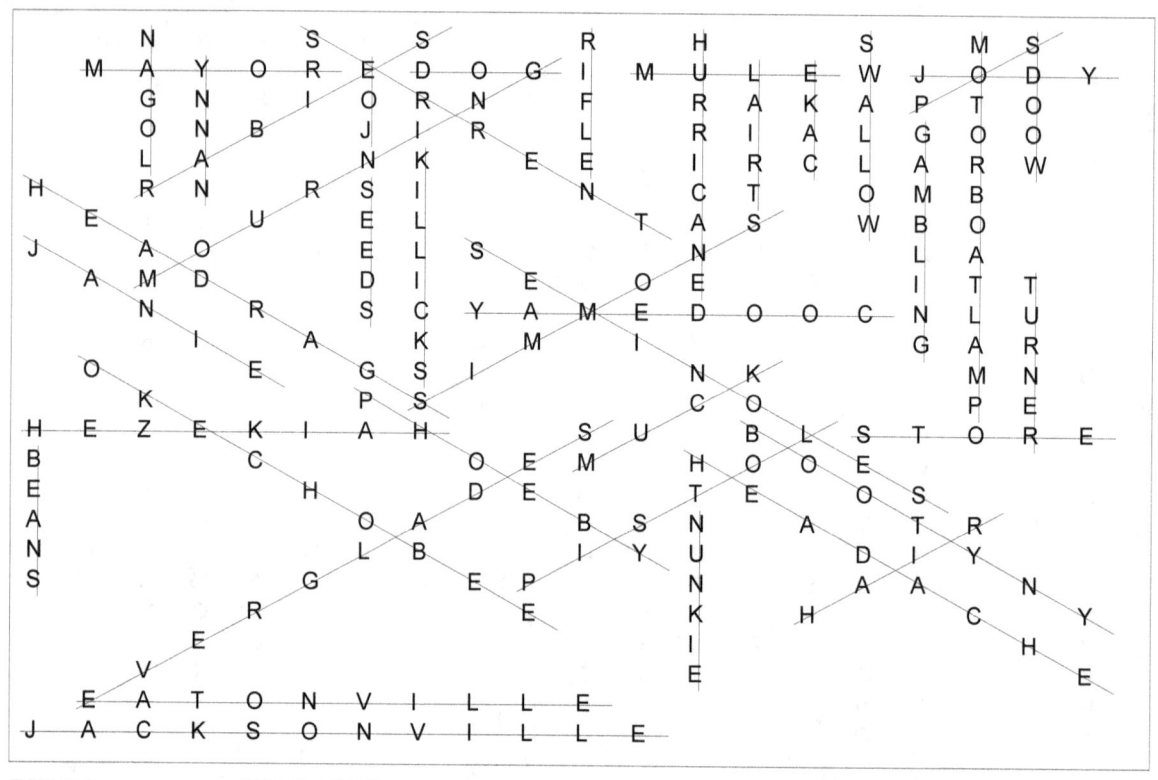

BEANS	HEADACHE	LAMP	OKECHOBEE	SOP
BOOTYNY	HEADRAGS	LOGAN	PHOEBY	STORE
CAKE	HEZEKIAH	MAYOR	PISTOL	SWALLOW
COODEMAY	HURRICANE	MOTORBOAT	RABIES	TRIAL
DOG	JACKSONVILLE	MOURNING	RIFLE	TURNER
EATONVILLE	JANIE	MUCK	SEEDS	WOODS
EVERGLADES	JODY	MULE	SEMINOLES	
GAMBLING	JOE	NANNY	SERRENT	
HAIR	KILLICKS	NUNKIE	SIMMONS	

Their Eyes Were Watching God Crossword 1

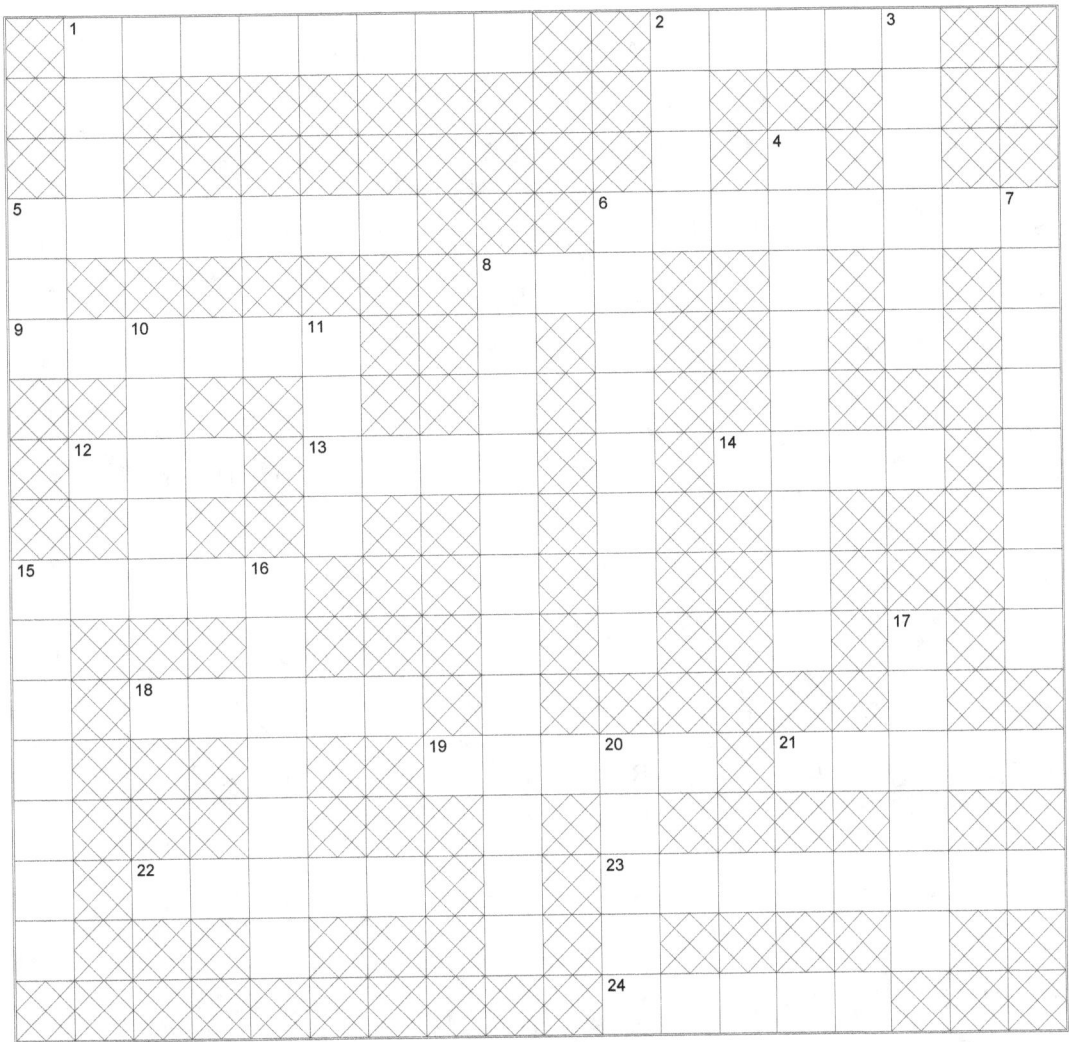

Across
1. Tea Cake tried to put him out of the restaurant
2. Joe was the first one in Eatonville
5. Drunken instigator of fight at the restaurant
6. Acted like Joe in the store
8. Janie's businessman-mayor husband
9. Tea Cake's weapon
12. Tea Cake killed it to save Janie
13. What Tea Cake called the Everglade crop land
14. Joe's nickname
15. Janie brought these back from the muck
18. Crop they picked on the muck
19. Janie's weapon
21. Narrator of the story
22. Vergible _____; Tea Cake
23. How Tea Cake got Janie's money back
24. Raised Janie

Down
1. Tea ____
2. Nanny compared the black woman to one
3. Disease Tea Cake got from dog
4. Janie watched a band of them leave the muck
5. Wanted to testify at Janie's trial: ___-de-Bottom
6. Joe made Janie wear them in the store
7. Tea Cake's first symptom
8. Site of Tea Cake and Janie's wedding
10. Joe started one in Eatonville
11. Town celebrated its installation; street ___
15. Doctor who testified in Janie's behalf
16. What Tea Cake couldn't do when he was sick
17. Made a play for Tea Cake
20. Mr. Killicks' first name

Their Eyes Were Watching God Crossword 1 Answer Key

Across
1. Tea Cake tried to put him out of the restaurant
2. Joe was the first one in Eatonville
5. Drunken instigator of fight at the restaurant
6. Acted like Joe in the store
8. Janie's businessman-mayor husband
9. Tea Cake's weapon
12. Tea Cake killed it to save Janie
13. What Tea Cake called the Everglade crop land
14. Joe's nickname
15. Janie brought these back from the muck
18. Crop they picked on the muck
19. Janie's weapon
21. Narrator of the story
22. Vergible _____; Tea Cake
23. How Tea Cake got Janie's money back
24. Raised Janie

Down
1. Tea _____
2. Nanny compared the black woman to one
3. Disease Tea Cake got from dog
4. Janie watched a band of them leave the muck
5. Wanted to testify at Janie's trial: _____-de-Bottom
6. Joe made Janie wear them in the store
7. Tea Cake's first symptom
8. Site of Tea Cake and Janie's wedding
10. Joe started one in Eatonville
11. Town celebrated its installation; street _____
15. Doctor who testified in Janie's behalf
16. What Tea Cake couldn't do when he was sick
17. Made a play for Tea Cake
20. Mr. Killicks' first name

Their Eyes Were Watching God Crossword 2

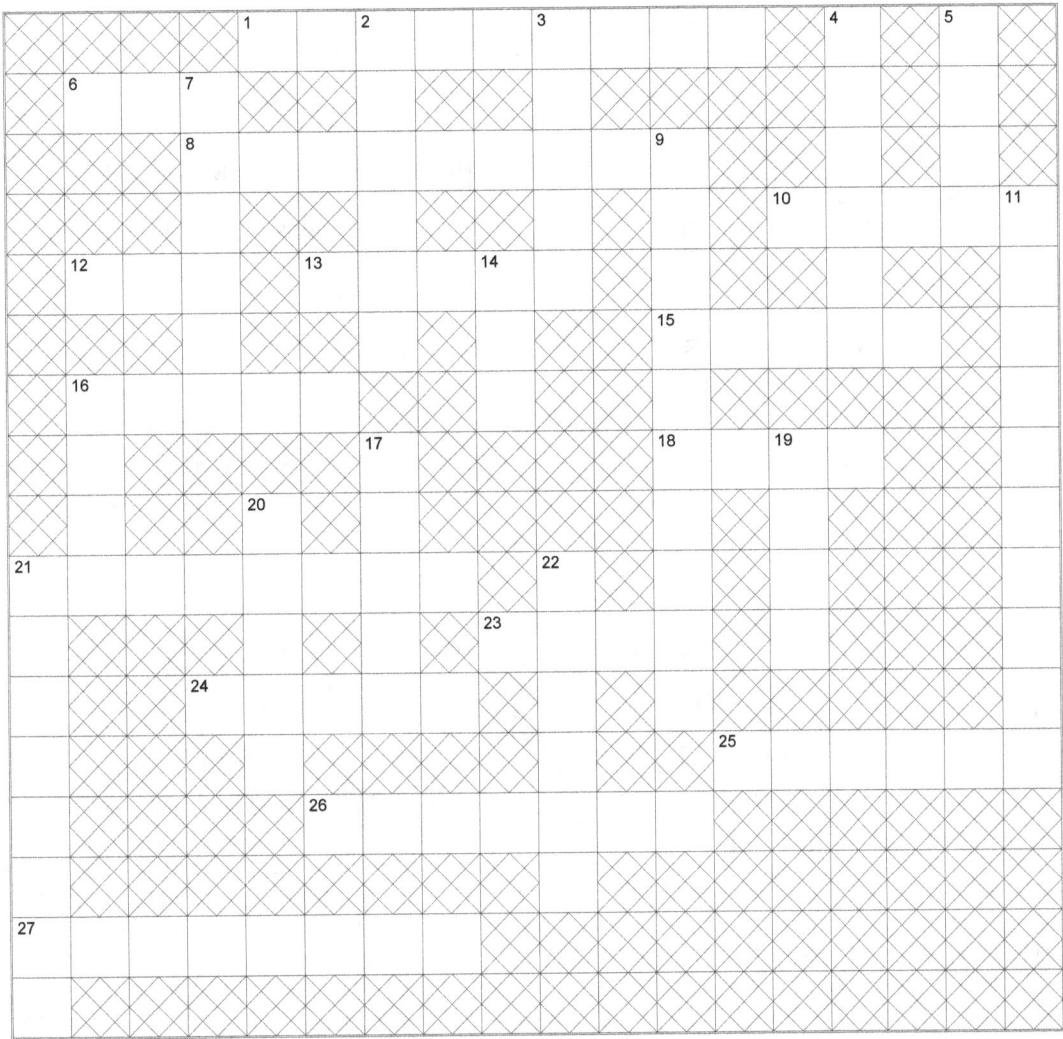

Across
1. Slept through the hurricane
6. Wanted to testify at Janie's trial: ___-de-Bottom
8. Caused evacuation of the muck
10. Joe started one in Eatonville
12. Janie's businessman-mayor husband
13. Janie brought these back from the muck
15. Janie's weapon
16. Joe was the first one in Eatonville
18. Town celebrated its installation; street ___
21. Joe made Janie wear them in the store
23. Tea ____
24. Raised Janie
25. Made a play for Tea Cake
26. Drunken instigator of fight at the restaurant
27. Acted like Joe in the store

Down
2. Mrs. ___ didn't like dark-skinned Blacks
3. Crop they picked on the muck
4. Tea Cake's weapon
5. Janie's most noticeable physical characteristic
7. First to hear Janie's story
9. Location of the muck
11. Town where Joe and Janie settled
14. Tea Cake killed it to save Janie
16. Nanny compared the black woman to one
17. Mr. Killicks' first name
19. What Tea Cake called the Everglade crop land
20. Held the same day as Tea Cake's death
21. Tea Cake's first symptom
22. Disease Tea Cake got from dog

Their Eyes Were Watching God Crossword 2 Answer Key

Across
1. Slept through the hurricane
6. Wanted to testify at Janie's trial: ___-de-Bottom
8. Caused evacuation of the muck
10. Joe started one in Eatonville
12. Janie's businessman-mayor husband
13. Janie brought these back from the muck
15. Janie's weapon
16. Joe was the first one in Eatonville
18. Town celebrated its installation; street ___
21. Joe made Janie wear them in the store
23. Tea ___
24. Raised Janie
25. Made a play for Tea Cake
26. Drunken instigator of fight at the restaurant
27. Acted like Joe in the store

Down
2. Mrs. ___ didn't like dark-skinned Blacks
3. Crop they picked on the muck
4. Tea Cake's weapon
5. Janie's most noticeable physical characteristic
7. First to hear Janie's story
9. Location of the muck
11. Town where Joe and Janie settled
14. Tea Cake killed it to save Janie
16. Nanny compared the black woman to one
17. Mr. Killicks' first name
19. What Tea Cake called the Everglade crop land
20. Held the same day as Tea Cake's death
21. Tea Cake's first symptom
22. Disease Tea Cake got from dog

Their Eyes Were Watching God Crossword 3

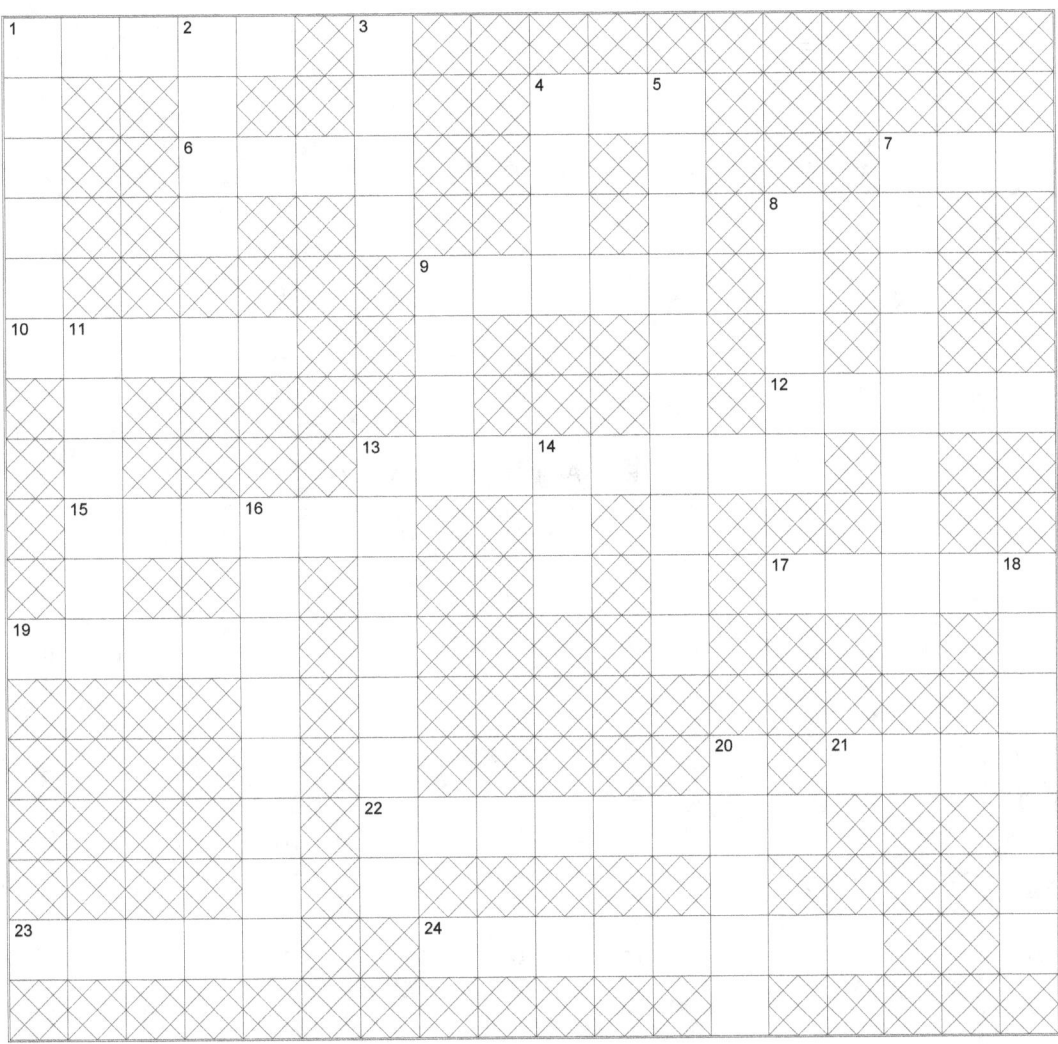

Across
1. Janie's weapon
4. Janie's businessman-mayor husband
6. What Tea Cake called the Everglade crop land
7. Wanted to testify at Janie's trial: ___-de-Bottom
9. Joe was the first one in Eatonville
10. Joe started one in Eatonville
12. Raised Janie
13. Joe made Janie wear them in the store
15. Made a play for Tea Cake
17. Janie brought these back from the muck
19. Held the same day as Tea Cake's death
21. Janie's most noticeable physical characteristic
22. Acted like Joe in the store
23. Vergible _____; Tea Cake
24. It shouldn't last any longer than grief

Down
1. Disease Tea Cake got from dog
2. Town celebrated its installation; street ___
3. Tea ____
4. Joe's nickname
5. Location of the muck
7. Janie watched a band of them leave the muck
8. Crop they picked on the muck
9. Nanny compared the black woman to one
11. Mrs. ___ didn't like dark-skinned Blacks
13. Tea Cake's first symptom
14. Tea Cake killed it to save Janie
16. Last name of Janie's farmer husband
18. Drunken instigator of fight at the restaurant
20. Narrator of the story

Their Eyes Were Watching God Crossword 3 Answer Key

	1	2	3	4	5	6	7
	R	I F L E	C				

(Crossword grid with the following filled answers)

Across:
1. RIFLE
4. JOE
6. MUCK
7. SOP
9. MAYOR
10. STORE
12. NANNY
13. HEADRAGS
15. NUNKIE
17. SEEDS
19. TRIAL
21. HAIR
22. HEZEKIAH
23. WOODS
24. MOURNING

Down:
1. RABIES
2.␣ (LAMP — PAVING?) — (LAMP)
3. CAKE
4. JODY
5. EVERGLADES
7. SOBEM (?)
8. BEANS
9. MULE
11. TURNER
13. HEADACHE
14. DOG
16. KILLICKS
18. SEMEN (?)
20. JANIE

Across
1. Janie's weapon
4. Janie's businessman-mayor husband
6. What Tea Cake called the Everglade crop land
7. Wanted to testify at Janie's trial: ___-de-Bottom
9. Joe was the first one in Eatonville
10. Joe started one in Eatonville
12. Raised Janie
13. Joe made Janie wear them in the store
15. Made a play for Tea Cake
17. Janie brought these back from the muck
19. Held the same day as Tea Cake's death
21. Janie's most noticeable physical characteristic
22. Acted like Joe in the store
23. Vergible _____; Tea Cake
24. It shouldn't last any longer than grief

Down
1. Disease Tea Cake got from dog
2. Town celebrated its installation; street ___
3. Tea ___
4. Joe's nickname
5. Location of the muck
7. Janie watched a band of them leave the muck
8. Crop they picked on the muck
9. Nanny compared the black woman to one
11. Mrs. ___ didn't like dark-skinned Blacks
13. Tea Cake's first symptom
14. Tea Cake killed it to save Janie
16. Last name of Janie's farmer husband
18. Drunken instigator of fight at the restaurant
20. Narrator of the story

Their Eyes Were Watching God Crossword 4

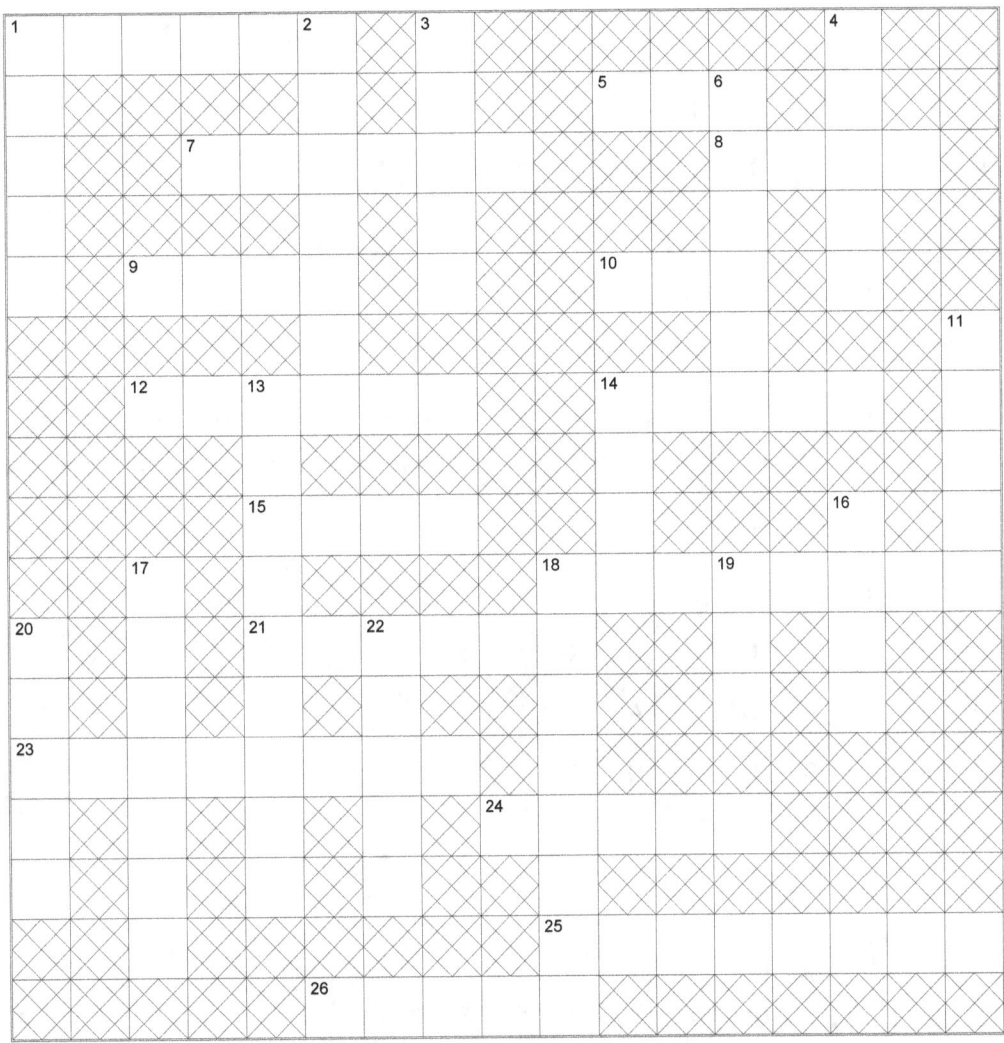

Across
1. Disease Tea Cake got from dog
5. Wanted to testify at Janie's trial: ___-de-Bottom
7. Mrs. ___ didn't like dark-skinned Blacks
8. Janie's most noticeable physical characteristic
9. Tea ____
10. Janie's businessman-mayor husband
12. Tea Cake's weapon
14. Joe was the first one in Eatonville
15. What Tea Cake called the Everglade crop land
18. Joe made Janie wear them in the store
21. Made a play for Tea Cake
23. How Tea Cake got Janie's money back
24. Narrator of the story
25. Acted like Joe in the store
26. Joe started one in Eatonville

Down
1. Janie's weapon
2. Drunken instigator of fight at the restaurant
3. Janie brought these back from the muck
4. Held the same day as Tea Cake's death
6. First to hear Janie's story
11. Crop they picked on the muck
13. Janie watched a band of them leave the muck
14. Nanny compared the black woman to one
16. Town celebrated its installation; street ___
17. Doctor who testified in Janie's behalf
18. Tea Cake's first symptom
19. Tea Cake killed it to save Janie
20. Mr. Killicks' first name
22. Raised Janie

Their Eyes Were Watching God Crossword 4 Answer Key

Across
1. Disease Tea Cake got from dog
5. Wanted to testify at Janie's trial: ___-de-Bottom
7. Mrs. ___ didn't like dark-skinned Blacks
8. Janie's most noticeable physical characteristic
9. Tea ___
10. Janie's businessman-mayor husband
12. Tea Cake's weapon
14. Joe was the first one in Eatonville
15. What Tea Cake called the Everglade crop land
18. Joe made Janie wear them in the store
21. Made a play for Tea Cake
23. How Tea Cake got Janie's money back
24. Narrator of the story
25. Acted like Joe in the store
26. Joe started one in Eatonville

Down
1. Janie's weapon
2. Drunken instigator of fight at the restaurant
3. Janie brought these back from the muck
4. Held the same day as Tea Cake's death
6. First to hear Janie's story
11. Crop they picked on the muck
13. Janie watched a band of them leave the muck
14. Nanny compared the black woman to one
16. Town celebrated its installation; street ___
17. Doctor who testified in Janie's behalf
18. Tea Cake's first symptom
19. Tea Cake killed it to save Janie
20. Mr. Killicks' first name
22. Raised Janie

Their Eyes Were Watching God

TRIAL	GAMBLING	DOG	COODEMAY	WOODS
OKECHOBEE	CAKE	EATONVILLE	HAIR	TURNER
SWALLOW	MOTORBOAT	FREE SPACE	LAMP	RIFLE
BOOTYNY	RABIES	JODY	SOP	JACKSONVILLE
SEEDS	MUCK	JANIE	SEMINOLES	EVERGLADES

Their Eyes Were Watching God

LOGAN	HURRICANE	KILLICKS	MOURNING	SIMMONS
MAYOR	PHOEBY	PISTOL	BEANS	SERRENT
HEADACHE	NUNKIE	FREE SPACE	HEZEKIAH	HEADRAGS
NANNY	JOE	EVERGLADES	SEMINOLES	JANIE
MUCK	SEEDS	JACKSONVILLE	SOP	JODY

Their Eyes Were Watching God

JODY	LOGAN	SEMINOLES	STORE	JANIE
COODEMAY	SEEDS	MOURNING	HAIR	JOE
BOOTYNY	SOP	FREE SPACE	TRIAL	MUCK
HURRICANE	BEANS	HEADRAGS	GAMBLING	JACKSONVILLE
TURNER	PISTOL	KILLICKS	RIFLE	HEZEKIAH

Their Eyes Were Watching God

NUNKIE	DOG	CAKE	HEADACHE	MAYOR
MULE	NANNY	EVERGLADES	MOTORBOAT	RABIES
OKECHOBEE	SERRENT	FREE SPACE	WOODS	PHOEBY
LAMP	SIMMONS	HEZEKIAH	RIFLE	KILLICKS
PISTOL	TURNER	JACKSONVILLE	GAMBLING	HEADRAGS

Their Eyes Were Watching God

HURRICANE	GAMBLING	MOTORBOAT	NANNY	JANIE
SWALLOW	OKECHOBEE	SEMINOLES	SERRENT	RABIES
STORE	TURNER	FREE SPACE	SIMMONS	EVERGLADES
JODY	DOG	EATONVILLE	SOP	MUCK
SEEDS	JACKSONVILLE	BEANS	BOOTYNY	JOE

Their Eyes Were Watching God

LAMP	LOGAN	PHOEBY	PISTOL	TRIAL
KILLICKS	NUNKIE	HEZEKIAH	HAIR	MAYOR
RIFLE	CAKE	FREE SPACE	HEADRAGS	HEADACHE
COODEMAY	MOURNING	JOE	BOOTYNY	BEANS
JACKSONVILLE	SEEDS	MUCK	SOP	EATONVILLE

Their Eyes Were Watching God

WOODS	OKECHOBEE	EVERGLADES	GAMBLING	JANIE
HURRICANE	MULE	COODEMAY	MUCK	SEEDS
RABIES	HEADRAGS	FREE SPACE	PISTOL	RIFLE
TRIAL	PHOEBY	SIMMONS	HEADACHE	DOG
CAKE	SWALLOW	TURNER	NANNY	NUNKIE

Their Eyes Were Watching God

JODY	JACKSONVILLE	LAMP	SEMINOLES	JOE
STORE	EATONVILLE	HEZEKIAH	LOGAN	BEANS
MOTORBOAT	MOURNING	FREE SPACE	SERRENT	MAYOR
KILLICKS	HAIR	NUNKIE	NANNY	TURNER
SWALLOW	CAKE	DOG	HEADACHE	SIMMONS

Their Eyes Were Watching God

BEANS	HEADRAGS	TRIAL	SIMMONS	HAIR
RABIES	EVERGLADES	HEADACHE	JANIE	NUNKIE
PISTOL	MUCK	FREE SPACE	MAYOR	SWALLOW
JODY	BOOTYNY	CAKE	JACKSONVILLE	STORE
MULE	OKECHOBEE	SEMINOLES	DOG	JOE

Their Eyes Were Watching God

WOODS	HEZEKIAH	COODEMAY	MOTORBOAT	HURRICANE
RIFLE	GAMBLING	PHOEBY	LAMP	SERRENT
SOP	KILLICKS	FREE SPACE	MOURNING	SEEDS
NANNY	EATONVILLE	JOE	DOG	SEMINOLES
OKECHOBEE	MULE	STORE	JACKSONVILLE	CAKE

Their Eyes Were Watching God

EVERGLADES	SEEDS	HEADRAGS	RIFLE	PISTOL
TURNER	HAIR	MULE	HURRICANE	JOE
SOP	KILLICKS	FREE SPACE	STORE	SERRENT
JACKSONVILLE	HEZEKIAH	OKECHOBEE	TRIAL	SWALLOW
MOTORBOAT	NUNKIE	MUCK	LAMP	DOG

Their Eyes Were Watching God

JANIE	COODEMAY	HEADACHE	SEMINOLES	RABIES
WOODS	BOOTYNY	BEANS	EATONVILLE	NANNY
MAYOR	PHOEBY	FREE SPACE	JODY	CAKE
MOURNING	LOGAN	DOG	LAMP	MUCK
NUNKIE	MOTORBOAT	SWALLOW	TRIAL	OKECHOBEE

Their Eyes Were Watching God

WOODS	BEANS	HURRICANE	EVERGLADES	STORE
COODEMAY	NUNKIE	SOP	JOE	BOOTYNY
LOGAN	MULE	FREE SPACE	MAYOR	JANIE
DOG	LAMP	HAIR	EATONVILLE	HEADACHE
JODY	SIMMONS	HEADRAGS	GAMBLING	HEZEKIAH

Their Eyes Were Watching God

CAKE	JACKSONVILLE	MOURNING	SERRENT	SWALLOW
OKECHOBEE	MOTORBOAT	PHOEBY	TURNER	RIFLE
KILLICKS	SEEDS	FREE SPACE	MUCK	SEMINOLES
RABIES	TRIAL	HEZEKIAH	GAMBLING	HEADRAGS
SIMMONS	JODY	HEADACHE	EATONVILLE	HAIR

Their Eyes Were Watching God

CAKE	KILLICKS	MOURNING	LAMP	HAIR
EATONVILLE	JODY	MOTORBOAT	GAMBLING	LOGAN
STORE	SEMINOLES	FREE SPACE	SEEDS	DOG
PHOEBY	BOOTYNY	RABIES	COODEMAY	JACKSONVILLE
SERRENT	SWALLOW	HEADACHE	TURNER	MULE

Their Eyes Were Watching God

JANIE	HURRICANE	BEANS	WOODS	EVERGLADES
SIMMONS	TRIAL	JOE	HEZEKIAH	PISTOL
OKECHOBEE	MAYOR	FREE SPACE	NANNY	NUNKIE
HEADRAGS	RIFLE	MULE	TURNER	HEADACHE
SWALLOW	SERRENT	JACKSONVILLE	COODEMAY	RABIES

Their Eyes Were Watching God

CAKE	SWALLOW	LAMP	HAIR	DOG
JANIE	HEADACHE	MULE	NUNKIE	MAYOR
NANNY	PISTOL	FREE SPACE	JODY	SOP
LOGAN	EATONVILLE	EVERGLADES	BEANS	JACKSONVILLE
HEADRAGS	SIMMONS	MUCK	SERRENT	TURNER

Their Eyes Were Watching God

SEMINOLES	MOTORBOAT	STORE	RIFLE	OKECHOBEE
RABIES	PHOEBY	COODEMAY	TRIAL	HEZEKIAH
SEEDS	MOURNING	FREE SPACE	BOOTYNY	WOODS
JOE	KILLICKS	TURNER	SERRENT	MUCK
SIMMONS	HEADRAGS	JACKSONVILLE	BEANS	EVERGLADES

Their Eyes Were Watching God

MAYOR	BEANS	SERRENT	RIFLE	HEADACHE
SEMINOLES	NUNKIE	OKECHOBEE	PISTOL	JOE
EATONVILLE	HEADRAGS	FREE SPACE	MOURNING	EVERGLADES
CAKE	SOP	BOOTYNY	NANNY	LOGAN
MULE	RABIES	SIMMONS	JODY	PHOEBY

Their Eyes Were Watching God

LAMP	MOTORBOAT	JACKSONVILLE	COODEMAY	MUCK
KILLICKS	TURNER	HEZEKIAH	STORE	SEEDS
TRIAL	JANIE	FREE SPACE	DOG	GAMBLING
WOODS	SWALLOW	PHOEBY	JODY	SIMMONS
RABIES	MULE	LOGAN	NANNY	BOOTYNY

Their Eyes Were Watching God

HEADRAGS	RIFLE	RABIES	JODY	COODEMAY
NUNKIE	JANIE	NANNY	HEADACHE	LOGAN
OKECHOBEE	JOE	FREE SPACE	HURRICANE	SIMMONS
JACKSONVILLE	TURNER	DOG	PHOEBY	HAIR
MOTORBOAT	STORE	HEZEKIAH	PISTOL	SEMINOLES

Their Eyes Were Watching God

SOP	SWALLOW	MOURNING	EATONVILLE	KILLICKS
MUCK	SERRENT	CAKE	BEANS	BOOTYNY
GAMBLING	MULE	FREE SPACE	EVERGLADES	LAMP
MAYOR	TRIAL	SEMINOLES	PISTOL	HEZEKIAH
STORE	MOTORBOAT	HAIR	PHOEBY	DOG

Their Eyes Were Watching God

CAKE	JACKSONVILLE	SEEDS	JODY	DOG
LAMP	COODEMAY	RABIES	HEADACHE	GAMBLING
WOODS	BEANS	FREE SPACE	HEZEKIAH	JANIE
SIMMONS	MAYOR	SWALLOW	EVERGLADES	NANNY
TRIAL	EATONVILLE	STORE	HURRICANE	KILLICKS

Their Eyes Were Watching God

SERRENT	PHOEBY	LOGAN	PISTOL	TURNER
JOE	RIFLE	MULE	BOOTYNY	MUCK
HAIR	OKECHOBEE	FREE SPACE	NUNKIE	MOTORBOAT
MOURNING	SOP	KILLICKS	HURRICANE	STORE
EATONVILLE	TRIAL	NANNY	EVERGLADES	SWALLOW

Their Eyes Were Watching God

BEANS	HEADRAGS	PISTOL	MAYOR	MOURNING
JOE	STORE	GAMBLING	KILLICKS	HAIR
PHOEBY	CAKE	FREE SPACE	SEEDS	MOTORBOAT
RIFLE	COODEMAY	TRIAL	NANNY	SWALLOW
TURNER	HURRICANE	SIMMONS	SEMINOLES	EATONVILLE

Their Eyes Were Watching God

OKECHOBEE	RABIES	LOGAN	SOP	LAMP
WOODS	JACKSONVILLE	DOG	NUNKIE	EVERGLADES
BOOTYNY	JODY	FREE SPACE	JANIE	HEZEKIAH
HEADACHE	MULE	EATONVILLE	SEMINOLES	SIMMONS
HURRICANE	TURNER	SWALLOW	NANNY	TRIAL

Their Eyes Were Watching God

STORE	GAMBLING	PISTOL	DOG	LOGAN
HURRICANE	LAMP	RABIES	TURNER	MOTORBOAT
SIMMONS	JANIE	FREE SPACE	SOP	PHOEBY
WOODS	JOE	HAIR	EATONVILLE	BOOTYNY
MOURNING	TRIAL	JACKSONVILLE	MUCK	SEMINOLES

Their Eyes Were Watching God

NUNKIE	HEADACHE	SEEDS	SERRENT	BEANS
COODEMAY	MAYOR	HEZEKIAH	NANNY	KILLICKS
MULE	SWALLOW	FREE SPACE	RIFLE	OKECHOBEE
EVERGLADES	CAKE	SEMINOLES	MUCK	JACKSONVILLE
TRIAL	MOURNING	BOOTYNY	EATONVILLE	HAIR

Their Eyes Were Watching God

SEMINOLES	EATONVILLE	OKECHOBEE	DOG	SEEDS
RIFLE	MAYOR	STORE	SIMMONS	NUNKIE
PISTOL	EVERGLADES	FREE SPACE	HEADACHE	HAIR
HURRICANE	LOGAN	SWALLOW	KILLICKS	BOOTYNY
NANNY	COODEMAY	JACKSONVILLE	MULE	LAMP

Their Eyes Were Watching God

PHOEBY	HEADRAGS	JODY	SOP	GAMBLING
RABIES	HEZEKIAH	MOURNING	BEANS	SERRENT
TURNER	MUCK	FREE SPACE	WOODS	MOTORBOAT
JOE	CAKE	LAMP	MULE	JACKSONVILLE
COODEMAY	NANNY	BOOTYNY	KILLICKS	SWALLOW

Their Eyes Were Watching God

JODY	KILLICKS	WOODS	RABIES	PISTOL
MOURNING	HURRICANE	NANNY	SWALLOW	TRIAL
MUCK	JACKSONVILLE	FREE SPACE	SOP	HEADRAGS
LOGAN	MOTORBOAT	SEMINOLES	JANIE	TURNER
EATONVILLE	SERRENT	OKECHOBEE	PHOEBY	SEEDS

Their Eyes Were Watching God

DOG	HEADACHE	JOE	HEZEKIAH	MULE
GAMBLING	STORE	COODEMAY	HAIR	SIMMONS
EVERGLADES	LAMP	FREE SPACE	CAKE	NUNKIE
RIFLE	BEANS	SEEDS	PHOEBY	OKECHOBEE
SERRENT	EATONVILLE	TURNER	JANIE	SEMINOLES

Their Eyes Were Watching God Vocabulary List

No.	Word	Clue/Definition
1.	BAITING	Taunting, teasing, luring
2.	BROACHED	Brought up for discussion
3.	COMPELLMENT	Strong urging forces
4.	CONJECTURES	Ideas formed from guessing
5.	CONSOLIDATED	United into one system; combined
6.	COSMIC	Universal; vast
7.	COWED	Bullied
8.	DELIRIUM	Mental confusion caused by illness
9.	DESECRATING	Violating the sacredness of
10.	DISENGAGED	Released; detached
11.	DISGORGED	Vomited; threw up
12.	DWINDLED	Became gradually smaller until nothing remained
13.	ENDURABLE	Able to be tolerated for a long time
14.	EULOGY	Speech or praise about a dead person
15.	EXCRUCIATING	Intensely painful; agonizing
16.	EXPOUND	Explain; give a detailed account
17.	FEND	Resist; push away
18.	FEROCITY	Savageness; fierceness
19.	FETID	Having an offensive odor
20.	FIEND	Bad or evil person
21.	FRACAS	A fight; a brawl
22.	FUTILE	Having no useful result
23.	GALLANTLY	Nobly; boldy
24.	GAPED	Opened wide
25.	HYPOCRITES	People who say one thing but do the opposite
26.	INCREDULOUS	Unbelieving; skeptical
27.	INEVITABLE	Unavoidable
28.	INSINUATIONS	Subtly made suggestions
29.	JURISDICTION	Area of control or power
30.	LACERATING	Ripping; cutting; tearing
31.	LANGUID	Lacking energy or vitality; weak
32.	LANGUISHED	Wasted away; weakened
33.	LUSTILY	Robustly; strongly
34.	MALICE	Extreme ill-will or spite
35.	MIEN	Manner or appearance
36.	OBLIQUE	Slanted
37.	PERSEVERANCE	Persistence; dogged trying
38.	PREDECESSOR	An ancestor; one who came before
39.	PROMINENCE	Widely known; being easily identified
40.	PROSTRATING	Bowing down in adoration or submission
41.	PUGNACIOUSLY	Combative in nature; belligerently; rebelliously
42.	REFRACTED	Deflected from a straight path
43.	RESIGNATION	Unresisting acceptance
44.	SACRILEGE	Against something sacred
45.	SAUNTERED	Strolled
46.	SODDEN	Soaked; saturated
47.	STOLID	Having little or no emotion
48.	SUBMISSION	Giving in to another
49.	SUBTLE	Difficult to detect
50.	SULLEN	Sulky; morose
51.	SULTRY	Very hot and humid

Their Eyes Were Watching God Vocabulary List

No.	Word	Clue/Definition
52.	SUPPLICATION	Plea; earnest request
53.	TEMPORIZED	Negotiated to gain time
54.	TRANSIENTS	People without permanent homes
55.	TREACHEROUS	Dangerous
56.	USURPER	One who grabs money or property
57.	VELOCITY	Speed
58.	WANTON	Cruel; merciless

Their Eyes Were Watching God Vocabulary Fill In The Blanks 1

_____ 1. An ancestor; one who came before

_____ 2. Unresisting acceptance

_____ 3. Difficult to detect

_____ 4. Bowing down in adoration or submission

_____ 5. One who grabs money or property

_____ 6. Opened wide

_____ 7. Bad or evil person

_____ 8. Strong urging forces

_____ 9. Bullied

_____ 10. Unavoidable

_____ 11. Slanted

_____ 12. Against something sacred

_____ 13. Having no useful result

_____ 14. Released; detached

_____ 15. Sulky; morose

_____ 16. Vomited; threw up

_____ 17. People who say one thing but do the opposite

_____ 18. A fight; a brawl

_____ 19. Having an offensive odor

_____ 20. Mental confusion caused by illness

Their Eyes Were Watching God Vocabulary Fill In The Blanks 1 Answer Key

PREDECESSOR	1. An ancestor; one who came before
RESIGNATION	2. Unresisting acceptance
SUBTLE	3. Difficult to detect
PROSTRATING	4. Bowing down in adoration or submission
USURPER	5. One who grabs money or property
GAPED	6. Opened wide
FIEND	7. Bad or evil person
COMPELLMENT	8. Strong urging forces
COWED	9. Bullied
INEVITABLE	10. Unavoidable
OBLIQUE	11. Slanted
SACRILEGE	12. Against something sacred
FUTILE	13. Having no useful result
DISENGAGED	14. Released; detached
SULLEN	15. Sulky; morose
DISGORGED	16. Vomited; threw up
HYPOCRITES	17. People who say one thing but do the opposite
FRACAS	18. A fight; a brawl
FETID	19. Having an offensive odor
DELIRIUM	20. Mental confusion caused by illness

Their Eyes Were Watching God Vocabulary Fill In The Blanks 2

_____ 1. Unbelieving; skeptical

_____ 2. Ideas formed from guessing

_____ 3. Negotiated to gain time

_____ 4. Cruel; merciless

_____ 5. Violating the sacredness of

_____ 6. One who grabs money or property

_____ 7. Persistence; dogged trying

_____ 8. Widely known; being easily identified

_____ 9. Speech or praise about a dead person

_____ 10. People who say one thing but do the opposite

_____ 11. United into one system; combined

_____ 12. Extreme ill-will or spite

_____ 13. Savageness; fierceness

_____ 14. Wasted away; weakened

_____ 15. Slanted

_____ 16. Difficult to detect

_____ 17. Vomited; threw up

_____ 18. Giving in to another

_____ 19. Resist; push away

_____ 20. Manner or appearance

Their Eyes Were Watching God Vocabulary Fill In The Blanks 2 Answer Key

INCREDULOUS	1. Unbelieving; skeptical
CONJECTURES	2. Ideas formed from guessing
TEMPORIZED	3. Negotiated to gain time
WANTON	4. Cruel; merciless
DESECRATING	5. Violating the sacredness of
USURPER	6. One who grabs money or property
PERSEVERANCE	7. Persistence; dogged trying
PROMINENCE	8. Widely known; being easily identified
EULOGY	9. Speech or praise about a dead person
HYPOCRITES	10. People who say one thing but do the opposite
CONSOLIDATED	11. United into one system; combined
MALICE	12. Extreme ill-will or spite
FEROCITY	13. Savageness; fierceness
LANGUISHED	14. Wasted away; weakened
OBLIQUE	15. Slanted
SUBTLE	16. Difficult to detect
DISGORGED	17. Vomited; threw up
SUBMISSION	18. Giving in to another
FEND	19. Resist; push away
MIEN	20. Manner or appearance

Their Eyes Were Watching God Vocabulary Fill In The Blanks 3

1. One who grabs money or property
2. Mental confusion caused by illness
3. Negotiated to gain time
4. Brought up for discussion
5. People without permanent homes
6. United into one system; combined
7. Bowing down in adoration or submission
8. Resist; push away
9. Subtly made suggestions
10. Deflected from a straight path
11. Unavoidable
12. Opened wide
13. Plea; earnest request
14. Bad or evil person
15. Savageness; fierceness
16. Unbelieving; skeptical
17. Extreme ill-will or spite
18. Sulky; morose
19. Combative in nature; belligerently; rebelliously
20. Having an offensive odor

Their Eyes Were Watching God Vocabulary Fill In The Blanks 3 Answer Key

USURPER	1. One who grabs money or property
DELIRIUM	2. Mental confusion caused by illness
TEMPORIZED	3. Negotiated to gain time
BROACHED	4. Brought up for discussion
TRANSIENTS	5. People without permanent homes
CONSOLIDATED	6. United into one system; combined
PROSTRATING	7. Bowing down in adoration or submission
FEND	8. Resist; push away
INSINUATIONS	9. Subtly made suggestions
REFRACTED	10. Deflected from a straight path
INEVITABLE	11. Unavoidable
GAPED	12. Opened wide
SUPPLICATION	13. Plea; earnest request
FIEND	14. Bad or evil person
FEROCITY	15. Savageness; fierceness
INCREDULOUS	16. Unbelieving; skeptical
MALICE	17. Extreme ill-will or spite
SULLEN	18. Sulky; morose
PUGNACIOUSLY	19. Combative in nature; belligerently; rebelliously
FETID	20. Having an offensive odor

Their Eyes Were Watching God Vocabulary Fill In The Blanks 4

_____ 1. Violating the sacredness of

_____ 2. Lacking energy or vitality; weak

_____ 3. Strong urging forces

_____ 4. Robustly; strongly

_____ 5. Unbelieving; skeptical

_____ 6. Against something sacred

_____ 7. Sulky; morose

_____ 8. Brought up for discussion

_____ 9. Wasted away; weakened

_____ 10. Intensely painful; agonizing

_____ 11. Bowing down in adoration or submission

_____ 12. Area of control or power

_____ 13. Able to be tolerated for a long time

_____ 14. Cruel; merciless

_____ 15. United into one system; combined

_____ 16. Speed

_____ 17. Bullied

_____ 18. Extreme ill-will or spite

_____ 19. Soaked; saturated

_____ 20. Having no useful result

Their Eyes Were Watching God Vocabulary Fill In The Blanks 4 Answer Key

DESECRATING	1. Violating the sacredness of
LANGUID	2. Lacking energy or vitality; weak
COMPELLMENT	3. Strong urging forces
LUSTILY	4. Robustly; strongly
INCREDULOUS	5. Unbelieving; skeptical
SACRILEGE	6. Against something sacred
SULLEN	7. Sulky; morose
BROACHED	8. Brought up for discussion
LANGUISHED	9. Wasted away; weakened
EXCRUCIATING	10. Intensely painful; agonizing
PROSTRATING	11. Bowing down in adoration or submission
JURISDICTION	12. Area of control or power
ENDURABLE	13. Able to be tolerated for a long time
WANTON	14. Cruel; merciless
CONSOLIDATED	15. United into one system; combined
VELOCITY	16. Speed
COWED	17. Bullied
MALICE	18. Extreme ill-will or spite
SODDEN	19. Soaked; saturated
FUTILE	20. Having no useful result

Their Eyes Were Watching God Vocabulary Matching 1

1. GAPED — A. Bad or evil person
2. LANGUID — B. An ancestor; one who came before
3. EXCRUCIATING — C. Slanted
4. INCREDULOUS — D. Intensely painful; agonizing
5. STOLID — E. Area of control or power
6. OBLIQUE — F. Widely known; being easily identified
7. PREDECESSOR — G. Opened wide
8. MALICE — H. Able to be tolerated for a long time
9. SAUNTERED — I. Extreme ill-will or spite
10. CONJECTURES — J. Having little or no emotion
11. FIEND — K. Unbelieving; skeptical
12. LACERATING — L. Strolled
13. ENDURABLE — M. Ideas formed from guessing
14. FRACAS — N. Brought up for discussion
15. JURISDICTION — O. A fight; a brawl
16. WANTON — P. Sulky; morose
17. FETID — Q. Unavoidable
18. SUBTLE — R. Explain; give a detailed account
19. BROACHED — S. Cruel; merciless
20. PERSEVERANCE — T. Having an offensive odor
21. PROMINENCE — U. Ripping; cutting; tearing
22. INEVITABLE — V. Persistence; dogged trying
23. SULLEN — W. Unresisting acceptance
24. EXPOUND — X. Difficult to detect
25. RESIGNATION — Y. Lacking energy or vitality; weak

Their Eyes Were Watching God Vocabulary Matching 1 Answer Key

G - 1. GAPED
Y - 2. LANGUID
D - 3. EXCRUCIATING
K - 4. INCREDULOUS
J - 5. STOLID
C - 6. OBLIQUE
B - 7. PREDECESSOR
I - 8. MALICE
L - 9. SAUNTERED
M - 10. CONJECTURES
A - 11. FIEND
U - 12. LACERATING
H - 13. ENDURABLE
O - 14. FRACAS
E - 15. JURISDICTION
S - 16. WANTON
T - 17. FETID
X - 18. SUBTLE
N - 19. BROACHED
V - 20. PERSEVERANCE
F - 21. PROMINENCE
Q - 22. INEVITABLE
P - 23. SULLEN
R - 24. EXPOUND
W - 25. RESIGNATION

A. Bad or evil person
B. An ancestor; one who came before
C. Slanted
D. Intensely painful; agonizing
E. Area of control or power
F. Widely known; being easily identified
G. Opened wide
H. Able to be tolerated for a long time
I. Extreme ill-will or spite
J. Having little or no emotion
K. Unbelieving; skeptical
L. Strolled
M. Ideas formed from guessing
N. Brought up for discussion
O. A fight; a brawl
P. Sulky; morose
Q. Unavoidable
R. Explain; give a detailed account
S. Cruel; merciless
T. Having an offensive odor
U. Ripping; cutting; tearing
V. Persistence; dogged trying
W. Unresisting acceptance
X. Difficult to detect
Y. Lacking energy or vitality; weak

Their Eyes Were Watching God Vocabulary Matching 2

___ 1. COSMIC   A. Unavoidable
___ 2. COWED   B. Dangerous
___ 3. LUSTILY   C. Universal; vast
___ 4. INEVITABLE   D. Nobly; boldy
___ 5. FUTILE   E. People without permanent homes
___ 6. DELIRIUM   F. Brought up for discussion
___ 7. PERSEVERANCE   G. Explain; give a detailed account
___ 8. BROACHED   H. Speed
___ 9. EULOGY   I. Ideas formed from guessing
___10. STOLID   J. Opened wide
___11. SULLEN   K. Speech or praise about a dead person
___12. WANTON   L. Savageness; fierceness
___13. TREACHEROUS   M. Mental confusion caused by illness
___14. COMPELLMENT   N. Sulky; morose
___15. FEROCITY   O. Strong urging forces
___16. GAPED   P. Robustly; strongly
___17. SUBMISSION   Q. Cruel; merciless
___18. RESIGNATION   R. Unresisting acceptance
___19. MALICE   S. Very hot and humid
___20. EXPOUND   T. Extreme ill-will or spite
___21. TRANSIENTS   U. Having no useful result
___22. SULTRY   V. Bullied
___23. VELOCITY   W. Persistence; dogged trying
___24. GALLANTLY   X. Giving in to another
___25. CONJECTURES   Y. Having little or no emotion

Their Eyes Were Watching God Vocabulary Matching 2 Answer Key

C - 1. COSMIC	A. Unavoidable
V - 2. COWED	B. Dangerous
P - 3. LUSTILY	C. Universal; vast
A - 4. INEVITABLE	D. Nobly; boldy
U - 5. FUTILE	E. People without permanent homes
M - 6. DELIRIUM	F. Brought up for discussion
W - 7. PERSEVERANCE	G. Explain; give a detailed account
F - 8. BROACHED	H. Speed
K - 9. EULOGY	I. Ideas formed from guessing
Y - 10. STOLID	J. Opened wide
N - 11. SULLEN	K. Speech or praise about a dead person
Q - 12. WANTON	L. Savageness; fierceness
B - 13. TREACHEROUS	M. Mental confusion caused by illness
O - 14. COMPELLMENT	N. Sulky; morose
L - 15. FEROCITY	O. Strong urging forces
J - 16. GAPED	P. Robustly; strongly
X - 17. SUBMISSION	Q. Cruel; merciless
R - 18. RESIGNATION	R. Unresisting acceptance
T - 19. MALICE	S. Very hot and humid
G - 20. EXPOUND	T. Extreme ill-will or spite
E - 21. TRANSIENTS	U. Having no useful result
S - 22. SULTRY	V. Bullied
H - 23. VELOCITY	W. Persistence; dogged trying
D - 24. GALLANTLY	X. Giving in to another
I - 25. CONJECTURES	Y. Having little or no emotion

Their Eyes Were Watching God Vocabulary Matching 3

___ 1. CONJECTURES	A. Strong urging forces
___ 2. ENDURABLE	B. Opened wide
___ 3. FUTILE	C. Speech or praise about a dead person
___ 4. OBLIQUE	D. Area of control or power
___ 5. DISENGAGED	E. Deflected from a straight path
___ 6. REFRACTED	F. Cruel; merciless
___ 7. EULOGY	G. One who grabs money or property
___ 8. SUBTLE	H. Able to be tolerated for a long time
___ 9. LUSTILY	I. Difficult to detect
___ 10. RESIGNATION	J. Released; detached
___ 11. COWED	K. Strolled
___ 12. GAPED	L. Ideas formed from guessing
___ 13. HYPOCRITES	M. Bullied
___ 14. JURISDICTION	N. Having an offensive odor
___ 15. MIEN	O. Nobly; boldy
___ 16. COMPELLMENT	P. Slanted
___ 17. GALLANTLY	Q. Intensely painful; agonizing
___ 18. USURPER	R. Unbelieving; skeptical
___ 19. FETID	S. People who say one thing but do the opposite
___ 20. LANGUISHED	T. Unresisting acceptance
___ 21. WANTON	U. Wasted away; weakened
___ 22. SAUNTERED	V. Robustly; strongly
___ 23. COSMIC	W. Universal; vast
___ 24. INCREDULOUS	X. Having no useful result
___ 25. EXCRUCIATING	Y. Manner or appearance

Their Eyes Were Watching God Vocabulary Matching 3 Answer Key

L - 1. CONJECTURES		A. Strong urging forces
H - 2. ENDURABLE		B. Opened wide
X - 3. FUTILE		C. Speech or praise about a dead person
P - 4. OBLIQUE		D. Area of control or power
J - 5. DISENGAGED		E. Deflected from a straight path
E - 6. REFRACTED		F. Cruel; merciless
C - 7. EULOGY		G. One who grabs money or property
I - 8. SUBTLE		H. Able to be tolerated for a long time
V - 9. LUSTILY		I. Difficult to detect
T - 10. RESIGNATION		J. Released; detached
M - 11. COWED		K. Strolled
B - 12. GAPED		L. Ideas formed from guessing
S - 13. HYPOCRITES		M. Bullied
D - 14. JURISDICTION		N. Having an offensive odor
Y - 15. MIEN		O. Nobly; boldy
A - 16. COMPELLMENT		P. Slanted
O - 17. GALLANTLY		Q. Intensely painful; agonizing
G - 18. USURPER		R. Unbelieving; skeptical
N - 19. FETID		S. People who say one thing but do the opposite
U - 20. LANGUISHED		T. Unresisting acceptance
F - 21. WANTON		U. Wasted away; weakened
K - 22. SAUNTERED		V. Robustly; strongly
W - 23. COSMIC		W. Universal; vast
R - 24. INCREDULOUS		X. Having no useful result
Q - 25. EXCRUCIATING		Y. Manner or appearance

Their Eyes Were Watching God Vocabulary Matching 4

___ 1. PROMINENCE A. Savageness; fierceness
___ 2. PUGNACIOUSLY B. Negotiated to gain time
___ 3. WANTON C. Ideas formed from guessing
___ 4. DISGORGED D. Deflected from a straight path
___ 5. GALLANTLY E. Violating the sacredness of
___ 6. INSINUATIONS F. An ancestor; one who came before
___ 7. EULOGY G. Robustly; strongly
___ 8. TEMPORIZED H. Speed
___ 9. INCREDULOUS I. Unbelieving; skeptical
___ 10. OBLIQUE J. Combative in nature; belligerently; rebelliously
___ 11. REFRACTED K. Cruel; merciless
___ 12. VELOCITY L. Persistence; dogged trying
___ 13. COMPELLMENT M. Strong urging forces
___ 14. STOLID N. Slanted
___ 15. DISENGAGED O. Giving in to another
___ 16. FEROCITY P. Dangerous
___ 17. LUSTILY Q. Widely known; being easily identified
___ 18. TREACHEROUS R. Vomited; threw up
___ 19. LANGUID S. Having little or no emotion
___ 20. DESECRATING T. Subtly made suggestions
___ 21. FIEND U. Nobly; boldy
___ 22. CONJECTURES V. Released; detached
___ 23. SUBMISSION W. Speech or praise about a dead person
___ 24. PREDECESSOR X. Bad or evil person
___ 25. PERSEVERANCE Y. Lacking energy or vitality; weak

Their Eyes Were Watching God Vocabulary Matching 4 Answer Key

Q - 1.	PROMINENCE	A.	Savageness; fierceness
J - 2.	PUGNACIOUSLY	B.	Negotiated to gain time
K - 3.	WANTON	C.	Ideas formed from guessing
R - 4.	DISGORGED	D.	Deflected from a straight path
U - 5.	GALLANTLY	E.	Violating the sacredness of
T - 6.	INSINUATIONS	F.	An ancestor; one who came before
W - 7.	EULOGY	G.	Robustly; strongly
B - 8.	TEMPORIZED	H.	Speed
I - 9.	INCREDULOUS	I.	Unbelieving; skeptical
N - 10.	OBLIQUE	J.	Combative in nature; belligerently; rebelliously
D - 11.	REFRACTED	K.	Cruel; merciless
H - 12.	VELOCITY	L.	Persistence; dogged trying
M - 13.	COMPELLMENT	M.	Strong urging forces
S - 14.	STOLID	N.	Slanted
V - 15.	DISENGAGED	O.	Giving in to another
A - 16.	FEROCITY	P.	Dangerous
G - 17.	LUSTILY	Q.	Widely known; being easily identified
P - 18.	TREACHEROUS	R.	Vomited; threw up
Y - 19.	LANGUID	S.	Having little or no emotion
E - 20.	DESECRATING	T.	Subtly made suggestions
X - 21.	FIEND	U.	Nobly; boldy
C - 22.	CONJECTURES	V.	Released; detached
O - 23.	SUBMISSION	W.	Speech or praise about a dead person
F - 24.	PREDECESSOR	X.	Bad or evil person
L - 25.	PERSEVERANCE	Y.	Lacking energy or vitality; weak

Their Eyes Were Watching God Vocabulary Magic Squares 1

Match the definition with the vocabulary word. Put your answers in the magic squares below. When your answers are correct, all columns and rows will add to the same number.

A. FEND
B. SULLEN
C. SUPPLICATION
D. MIEN
E. SODDEN
F. EXPOUND
G. FEROCITY
H. SUBTLE
I. PUGNACIOUSLY
J. GAPED
K. EULOGY
L. FETID
M. TRANSIENTS
N. FRACAS
O. ENDURABLE
P. PROSTRATING

1. Plea; earnest request
2. Opened wide
3. Explain; give a detailed account
4. Able to be tolerated for a long time
5. Bowing down in adoration or submission
6. Soaked; saturated
7. Combative in nature; belligerently; rebelliously
8. Manner or appearance
9. People without permanent homes
10. Difficult to detect
11. Having an offensive odor
12. Resist; push away
13. Sulky; morose
14. Speech or praise about a dead person
15. Savageness; fierceness
16. A fight; a brawl

A=	B=	C=	D=
E=	F=	G=	H=
I=	J=	K=	L=
M=	N=	O=	P=

Their Eyes Were Watching God Vocabulary Magic Squares 1 Answer Key

Match the definition with the vocabulary word. Put your answers in the magic squares below. When your answers are correct, all columns and rows will add to the same number.

A. FEND
B. SULLEN
C. SUPPLICATION
D. MIEN
E. SODDEN
F. EXPOUND
G. FEROCITY
H. SUBTLE
I. PUGNACIOUSLY
J. GAPED
K. EULOGY
L. FETID
M. TRANSIENTS
N. FRACAS
O. ENDURABLE
P. PROSTRATING

1. Plea; earnest request
2. Opened wide
3. Explain; give a detailed account
4. Able to be tolerated for a long time
5. Bowing down in adoration or submission
6. Soaked; saturated
7. Combative in nature; belligerently; rebelliously
8. Manner or appearance
9. People without permanent homes
10. Difficult to detect
11. Having an offensive odor
12. Resist; push away
13. Sulky; morose
14. Speech or praise about a dead person
15. Savageness; fierceness
16. A fight; a brawl

A=12	B=13	C=1	D=8
E=6	F=3	G=15	H=10
I=7	J=2	K=14	L=11
M=9	N=16	O=4	P=5

Their Eyes Were Watching God Vocabulary Magic Squares 2

Match the definition with the vocabulary word. Put your answers in the magic squares below. When your answers are correct, all columns and rows will add to the same number.

A. SUBTLE
B. EXPOUND
C. FRACAS
D. DISGORGED
E. PUGNACIOUSLY
F. SUBMISSION
G. COMPELLMENT
H. EULOGY
I. MIEN
J. TRANSIENTS
K. HYPOCRITES
L. PROMINENCE
M. USURPER
N. CONSOLIDATED
O. PREDECESSOR
P. SULLEN

1. Speech or praise about a dead person
2. Difficult to detect
3. Explain; give a detailed account
4. Strong urging forces
5. People without permanent homes
6. An ancestor; one who came before
7. Sulky; morose
8. Manner or appearance
9. People who say one thing but do the opposite
10. United into one system; combined
11. One who grabs money or property
12. Widely known; being easily identified
13. Combative in nature; belligerently; rebelliously
14. Vomited; threw up
15. A fight; a brawl
16. Giving in to another

A= 2	B= 3	C= 15	D= 14
E= 13	F= 16	G= 4	H= 1
I= 8	J= 5	K= 9	L= 12
M= 11	N= 10	O= 6	P= 7

Their Eyes Were Watching God Vocabulary Magic Squares 2 Answer Key

Match the definition with the vocabulary word. Put your answers in the magic squares below. When your answers are correct, all columns and rows will add to the same number.

A. SUBTLE
B. EXPOUND
C. FRACAS
D. DISGORGED
E. PUGNACIOUSLY
F. SUBMISSION
G. COMPELLMENT
H. EULOGY
I. MIEN
J. TRANSIENTS
K. HYPOCRITES
L. PROMINENCE
M. USURPER
N. CONSOLIDATED
O. PREDECESSOR
P. SULLEN

1. Speech or praise about a dead person
2. Difficult to detect
3. Explain; give a detailed account
4. Strong urging forces
5. People without permanent homes
6. An ancestor; one who came before
7. Sulky; morose
8. Manner or appearance
9. People who say one thing but do the opposite
10. United into one system; combined
11. One who grabs money or property
12. Widely known; being easily identified
13. Combative in nature; belligerently; rebelliously
14. Vomited; threw up
15. A fight; a brawl
16. Giving in to another

A=2	B=3	C=15	D=14
E=13	F=16	G=4	H=1
I=8	J=5	K=9	L=12
M=11	N=10	O=6	P=7

Their Eyes Were Watching God Vocabulary Magic Squares 3

Match the definition with the vocabulary word. Put your answers in the magic squares below. When your answers are correct, all columns and rows will add to the same number.

A. TRANSIENTS	E. SULTRY	I. LUSTILY	M. MALICE
B. BROACHED	F. DELIRIUM	J. JURISDICTION	N. CONJECTURES
C. LANGUID	G. GAPED	K. MIEN	O. RESIGNATION
D. HYPOCRITES	H. SAUNTERED	L. SUBMISSION	P. COMPELLMENT

1. Ideas formed from guessing
2. Opened wide
3. Giving in to another
4. People without permanent homes
5. Manner or appearance
6. Brought up for discussion
7. Extreme ill-will or spite
8. Strolled
9. Very hot and humid
10. Strong urging forces
11. Lacking energy or vitality; weak
12. Area of control or power
13. People who say one thing but do the opposite
14. Robustly; strongly
15. Mental confusion caused by illness
16. Unresisting acceptance

A=	B=	C=	D=
E=	F=	G=	H=
I=	J=	K=	L=
M=	N=	O=	P=

Their Eyes Were Watching God Vocabulary Magic Squares 3 Answer Key

Match the definition with the vocabulary word. Put your answers in the magic squares below. When your answers are correct, all columns and rows will add to the same number.

A. TRANSIENTS   E. SULTRY   I. LUSTILY   M. MALICE
B. BROACHED   F. DELIRIUM   J. JURISDICTION   N. CONJECTURES
C. LANGUID   G. GAPED   K. MIEN   O. RESIGNATION
D. HYPOCRITES H. SAUNTERED   L. SUBMISSION   P. COMPELLMENT

1. Ideas formed from guessing
2. Opened wide
3. Giving in to another
4. People without permanent homes
5. Manner or appearance
6. Brought up for discussion
7. Extreme ill-will or spite
8. Strolled
9. Very hot and humid
10. Strong urging forces
11. Lacking energy or vitality; weak
12. Area of control or power
13. People who say one thing but do the opposite
14. Robustly; strongly
15. Mental confusion caused by illness
16. Unresisting acceptance

A=4	B=6	C=11	D=13
E=9	F=15	G=2	H=8
I=14	J=12	K=5	L=3
M=7	N=1	O=16	P=10

Their Eyes Were Watching God Vocabulary Magic Squares 4

Match the definition with the vocabulary word. Put your answers in the magic squares below. When your answers are correct, all columns and rows will add to the same number.

A. FETID
B. INEVITABLE
C. DISGORGED
D. VELOCITY
E. MALICE
F. CONSOLIDATED
G. BAITING
H. FEND
I. PERSEVERANCE
J. PROMINENCE
K. DISENGAGED
L. ENDURABLE
M. SULLEN
N. JURISDICTION
O. LACERATING
P. INCREDULOUS

1. Unavoidable
2. Taunting, teasing, luring
3. Released; detached
4. Area of control or power
5. Sulky; morose
6. Able to be tolerated for a long time
7. Resist; push away
8. Having an offensive odor
9. Unbelieving; skeptical
10. Persistence; dogged trying
11. Extreme ill-will or spite
12. Speed
13. Vomited; threw up
14. United into one system; combined
15. Widely known; being easily identified
16. Ripping; cutting; tearing

A=	B=	C=	D=
E=	F=	G=	H=
I=	J=	K=	L=
M=	N=	O=	P=

Their Eyes Were Watching God Vocabulary Magic Squares 4 Answer Key

Match the definition with the vocabulary word. Put your answers in the magic squares below. When your answers are correct, all columns and rows will add to the same number.

A. FETID
B. INEVITABLE
C. DISGORGED
D. VELOCITY
E. MALICE
F. CONSOLIDATED
G. BAITING
H. FEND
I. PERSEVERANCE
J. PROMINENCE
K. DISENGAGED
L. ENDURABLE
M. SULLEN
N. JURISDICTION
O. LACERATING
P. INCREDULOUS

1. Unavoidable
2. Taunting, teasing, luring
3. Released; detached
4. Area of control or power
5. Sulky; morose
6. Able to be tolerated for a long time
7. Resist; push away
8. Having an offensive odor
9. Unbelieving; skeptical
10. Persistence; dogged trying
11. Extreme ill-will or spite
12. Speed
13. Vomited; threw up
14. United into one system; combined
15. Widely known; being easily identified
16. Ripping; cutting; tearing

A=8	B=1	C=13	D=12
E=11	F=14	G=2	H=7
I=10	J=15	K=3	L=6
M=5	N=4	O=16	P=9

Their Eyes Were Watching God Vocabulary Word Search 1

Words are placed backwards, forward, diagonally, up and down. Clues listed below can help you find the words. Circle the hidden vocabulary words in the maze.

I	P	E	R	S	E	V	E	R	A	N	C	E	L	M	G	N	D	H	Q
N	S	M	P	L	A	N	G	U	I	S	H	E	D	A	M	D	E	Y	Z
S	A	Y	R	U	V	E	L	O	C	I	T	Y	Q	L	W	E	L	P	J
I	U	R	O	S	S	E	C	E	D	E	R	P	K	I	J	H	I	O	P
N	N	T	M	U	L	G	S	T	O	L	I	D	N	C	D	C	R	C	R
U	T	L	I	R	Z	E	U	L	O	G	Y	D	T	E	I	A	I	R	O
A	E	U	N	P	E	L	I	T	U	F	L	S	S	S	U	O	U	I	S
T	R	S	E	E	M	I	Y	D	D	E	E	D	U	T	G	R	M	T	T
I	E	W	N	R	V	R	D	E	D	R	E	E	L	Z	N	B	G	E	R
O	D	F	C	D	L	C	G	V	U	T	S	X	L	D	A	A	Y	S	A
N	M	I	E	N	P	A	D	T	C	O	M	P	E	L	L	M	E	N	T
S	J	P	R	N	G	S	C	A	P	D	F	O	N	L	Z	B	P	E	I
S	A	Q	P	N	D	E	R	E	S	E	Q	U	A	V	T	W	M	C	N
G	T	L	E	T	J	F	C	H	R	Q	C	N	Y	H	N	P	K	Z	G
H	B	S	C	N	E	Q	C	O	L	A	T	D	F	S	O	D	D	E	N
Z	I	A	O	R	S	F	C	U	S	L	T	D	Y	R	T	D	S	U	Y
D	V	C	I	A	X	I	S	X	Y	M	E	I	I	V	N	N	U	Q	D
J	L	T	C	T	T	T	D	M	P	W	I	Z	N	E	A	W	B	I	D
F	Q	A	S	Y	I	V	S	B	O	C	E	C	I	G	W	X	T	L	F
V	R	P	Z	L	W	N	J	C	H	D	J	F	K	B	D	E	L	B	K
F	G	N	Y	D	I	S	G	O	R	G	E	D	W	M	F	T	E	O	Y
V	S	F	Y	T	L	L	Z	J	C	D	Q	V	R	T	F	B	P	Y	F

A fight; a brawl (6)
Against something sacred (9)
An ancestor; one who came before (11)
Bad or evil person (5)
Became gradually smaller until nothing remained (8)
Bowing down in adoration or submission (11)
Brought up for discussion (8)
Bullied (5)
Cruel; merciless (6)
Deflected from a straight path (9)
Difficult to detect (6)
Explain; give a detailed account (7)
Extreme ill-will or spite (6)
Having an offensive odor (5)
Having little or no emotion (6)
Having no useful result (6)
Ideas formed from guessing (11)
Lacking energy or vitality; weak (7)
Manner or appearance (4)
Mental confusion caused by illness (8)
Negotiated to gain time (10)
Nobly; boldy (9)

One who grabs money or property (7)
Opened wide (5)
People who say one thing but do the opposite (10)
Persistence; dogged trying (12)
Released; detached (10)
Resist; push away (4)
Ripping; cutting; tearing (10)
Robustly; strongly (7)
Savageness; fierceness (8)
Slanted (7)
Soaked; saturated (6)
Speech or praise about a dead person (6)
Speed (8)
Strolled (9)
Strong urging forces (11)
Subtly made suggestions (12)
Sulky; morose (6)
Taunting, teasing, luring (7)
Universal; vast (6)
Very hot and humid (6)
Vomited; threw up (9)
Wasted away; weakened (10)
Widely known; being easily identified (10)

Their Eyes Were Watching God Vocabulary Word Search 1 Answer Key

Words are placed backwards, forward, diagonally, up and down. Clues listed below can help you find the words. Circle the hidden vocabulary words in the maze.

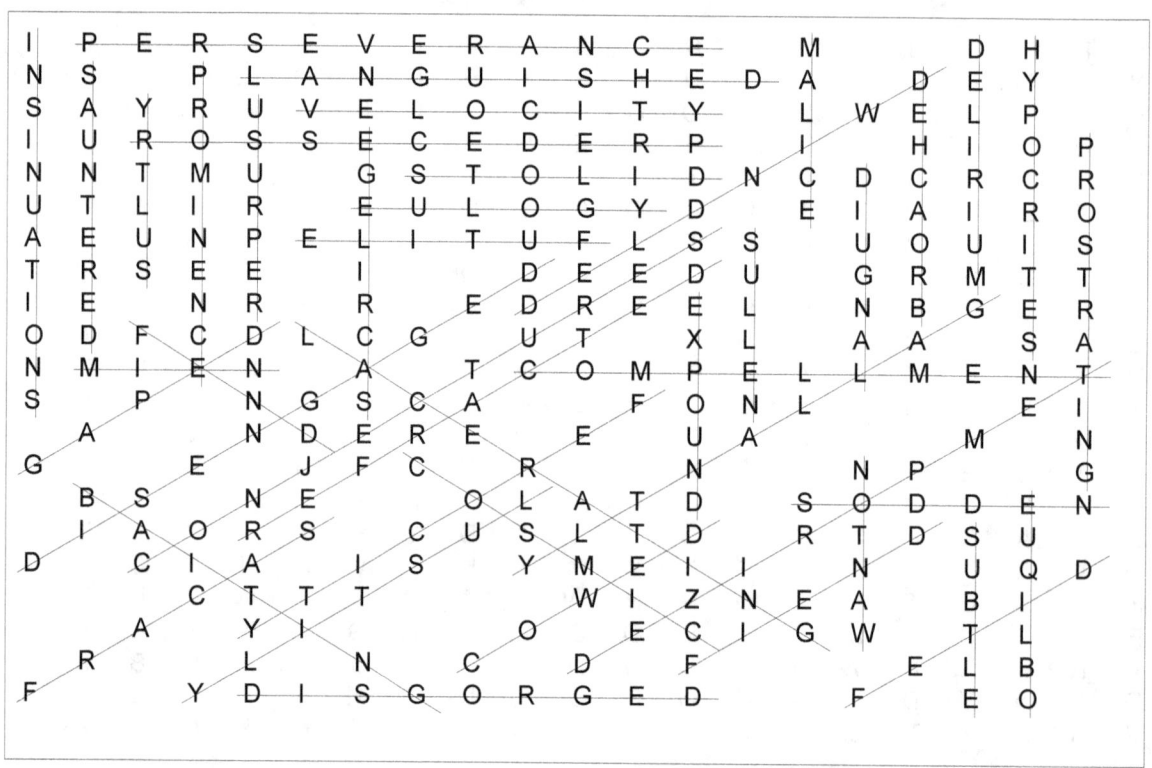

A fight; a brawl (6)
Against something sacred (9)
An ancestor; one who came before (11)
Bad or evil person (5)
Became gradually smaller until nothing remained (8)
Bowing down in adoration or submission (11)
Brought up for discussion (8)
Bullied (5)
Cruel; merciless (6)
Deflected from a straight path (9)
Difficult to detect (6)
Explain; give a detailed account (7)
Extreme ill-will or spite (6)
Having an offensive odor (5)
Having little or no emotion (6)
Having no useful result (6)
Ideas formed from guessing (11)
Lacking energy or vitality; weak (7)
Manner or appearance (4)
Mental confusion caused by illness (8)
Negotiated to gain time (10)
Nobly; boldy (9)

One who grabs money or property (7)
Opened wide (5)
People who say one thing but do the opposite (10)
Persistence; dogged trying (12)
Released; detached (10)
Resist; push away (4)
Ripping; cutting; tearing (10)
Robustly; strongly (7)
Savageness; fierceness (8)
Slanted (7)
Soaked; saturated (6)
Speech or praise about a dead person (6)
Speed (8)
Strolled (9)
Strong urging forces (11)
Subtly made suggestions (12)
Sulky; morose (6)
Taunting, teasing, luring (7)
Universal; vast (6)
Very hot and humid (6)
Vomited; threw up (9)
Wasted away; weakened (10)
Widely known; being easily identified (10)

Their Eyes Were Watching God Vocabulary Word Search 2

Words are placed backwards, forward, diagonally, up and down. Clues listed below can help you find the words. Circle the hidden vocabulary words in the maze.

```
I P E R S E V E R A N C E D M G T D H B
N S M P L A N G U I S H E D A L D E Y T
S A Y R U V E L O C I T Y Q L W E L P R
I U R O S S E C E D E R P D I W H I O P
N N T M U L G S T O L I D N C D C R C R
U T L I R N E U L O G Y D W E I A I R O
A E U N P E L I T U F L S S N U O U I S
T R S E E J I Z R D E E D U T G R M T T
I E G N R H Z E D R E E L X N B G E R A
O D F C D L C G X U T B X L V A A R S A
N M I E N P A Z T C O M P E L L M E N T
S H P L N G S C A S H F O N L T Q V E I
Q A R R N D E R E F E W U A F S J M N N
G R W E J J F C C R F V N N R N P B S G
V B S H N E V Q O L A T D P S O D D E N
Z I A O R S C C U S L T D G R T D S U P
D V C I A T I S K Y M E I I J N H U Q D
G V F C T T T K H G W I Z N E A L B I F
Q Q A N Y I D D H O J E C I G W N T L R
Q R D D L H N K C P D D F B H G E L B K
F C G Y D I S G O R G E D S S F C E O L
G T J N W G B K M S F P V P N Q J W T K
```

A fight; a brawl (6)
Against something sacred (9)
An ancestor; one who came before (11)
Bad or evil person (5)
Became gradually smaller until nothing remained (8)
Bowing down in adoration or submission (11)
Brought up for discussion (8)
Bullied (5)
Cruel; merciless (6)
Deflected from a straight path (9)
Difficult to detect (6)
Explain; give a detailed account (7)
Extreme ill-will or spite (6)
Having an offensive odor (5)
Having little or no emotion (6)
Having no useful result (6)
Ideas formed from guessing (11)
Lacking energy or vitality; weak (7)
Manner or appearance (4)
Mental confusion caused by illness (8)
Negotiated to gain time (10)
Nobly; boldy (9)

One who grabs money or property (7)
Opened wide (5)
People who say one thing but do the opposite (10)
Persistence; dogged trying (12)
Released; detached (10)
Resist; push away (4)
Ripping; cutting; tearing (10)
Robustly; strongly (7)
Savageness; fierceness (8)
Slanted (7)
Soaked; saturated (6)
Speech or praise about a dead person (6)
Speed (8)
Strolled (9)
Strong urging forces (11)
Subtly made suggestions (12)
Sulky; morose (6)
Taunting, teasing, luring (7)
Universal; vast (6)
Very hot and humid (6)
Vomited; threw up (9)
Wasted away; weakened (10)
Widely known; being easily identified (10)

Their Eyes Were Watching God Vocabulary Word Search 2 Answer Key

Words are placed backwards, forward, diagonally, up and down. Clues listed below can help you find the words. Circle the hidden vocabulary words in the maze.

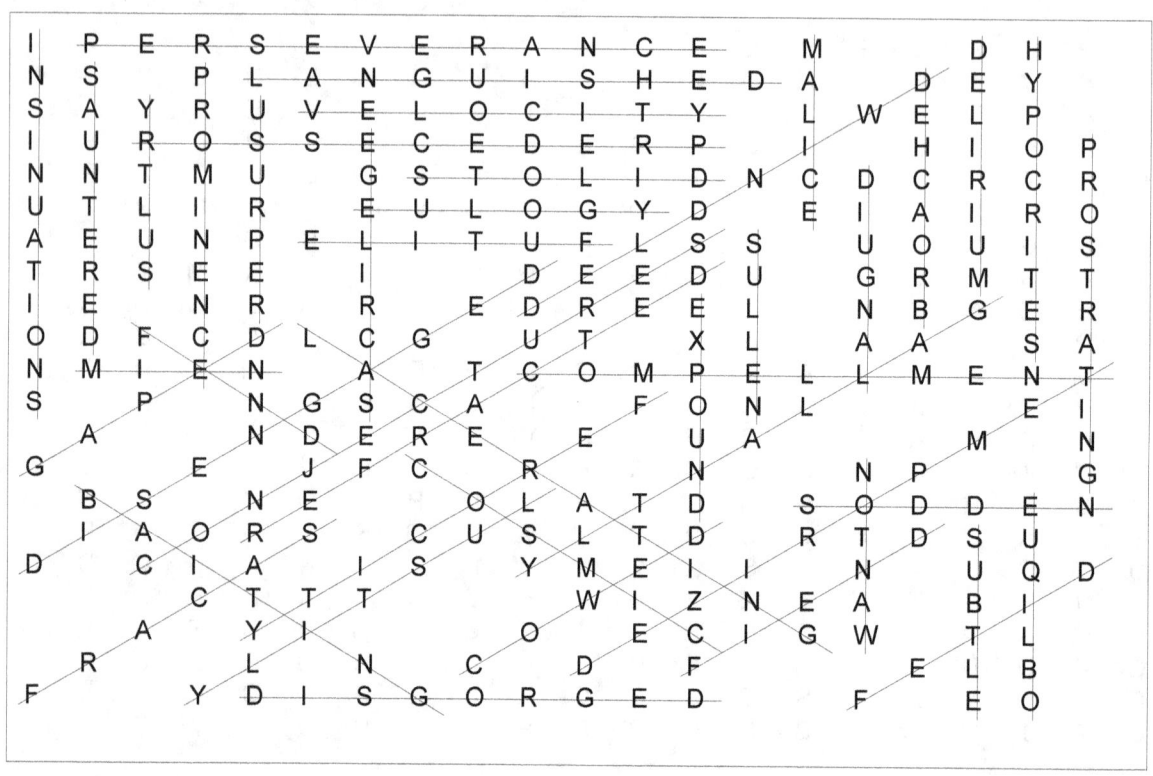

A fight; a brawl (6)
Against something sacred (9)
An ancestor; one who came before (11)
Bad or evil person (5)
Became gradually smaller until nothing remained (8)
Bowing down in adoration or submission (11)
Brought up for discussion (8)
Bullied (5)
Cruel; merciless (6)
Deflected from a straight path (9)
Difficult to detect (6)
Explain; give a detailed account (7)
Extreme ill-will or spite (6)
Having an offensive odor (5)
Having little or no emotion (6)
Having no useful result (6)
Ideas formed from guessing (11)
Lacking energy or vitality; weak (7)
Manner or appearance (4)
Mental confusion caused by illness (8)
Negotiated to gain time (10)
Nobly; boldy (9)

One who grabs money or property (7)
Opened wide (5)
People who say one thing but do the opposite (10)
Persistence; dogged trying (12)
Released; detached (10)
Resist; push away (4)
Ripping; cutting; tearing (10)
Robustly; strongly (7)
Savageness; fierceness (8)
Slanted (7)
Soaked; saturated (6)
Speech or praise about a dead person (6)
Speed (8)
Strolled (9)
Strong urging forces (11)
Subtly made suggestions (12)
Sulky; morose (6)
Taunting, teasing, luring (7)
Universal; vast (6)
Very hot and humid (6)
Vomited; threw up (9)
Wasted away; weakened (10)
Widely known; being easily identified (10)

Their Eyes Were Watching God Vocabulary Word Search 3

Words are placed backwards, forward, diagonally, up and down. Words listed below are included in the maze. Circle the hidden vocabulary words in the maze.

```
D E S E C R A T I N G Y R E P B S X V C
G J K X R R D F J L R I E N E P A G G R
T R E A C H E R O U S N F D L R C G D B
C Z V F Q S R W L S V S R U B O R M I Y
O B L I Q U E H D T X I A R A M I U S G
S V S P L S T C N I C N C A T I L I G L
U C K F O W N Z U L J U T B I N E R O R
L X T D F G U K O Y Q A E L V E G I R P
L D D B H Y A Z P B T T D E E N E L G G
E E U H G M S P X N R I L W N C Y E E D
N H S E R U T C E J N O C F I E N D D L
B H U J O H C M X D C N A M U N N R N V
A Z R K S V L T P I E S S C S T D K L S
I V P R S L R W T L Z O N Z H U I L X Z
T E E N E I M Y T I C O R E F E L L E P
I U R P C Q W B S J O L D E M E D T E D
N L M S E B U A S P W J N Y K A T Y R Q
G O M T D S C C N V E D G G Q S L I T Y
C G W X E A P J Z T D I U G N A L I D G
X Y R T R D E Z I R O P M E T R R M C M
G T F F P B R E S I G N A T I O N L Y E
S T O L I D S U B M I S S I O N W G S C
```

BAITING	DWINDLED	FUTILE	PREDECESSOR	SUBTLE
BROACHED	ENDURABLE	GAPED	PROMINENCE	SULLEN
COMPELLMENT	EULOGY	INEVITABLE	REFRACTED	SULTRY
CONJECTURES	EXPOUND	INSINUATIONS	RESIGNATION	TEMPORIZED
COSMIC	FEND	LANGUID	SACRILEGE	TREACHEROUS
COWED	FEROCITY	LUSTILY	SAUNTERED	USURPER
DELIRIUM	FETID	MALICE	SODDEN	VELOCITY
DESECRATING	FIEND	MIEN	STOLID	WANTON
DISGORGED	FRACAS	OBLIQUE	SUBMISSION	

Their Eyes Were Watching God Vocabulary Word Search 3 Answer Key

Words are placed backwards, forward, diagonally, up and down. Words listed below are included in the maze. Circle the hidden vocabulary words in the maze.

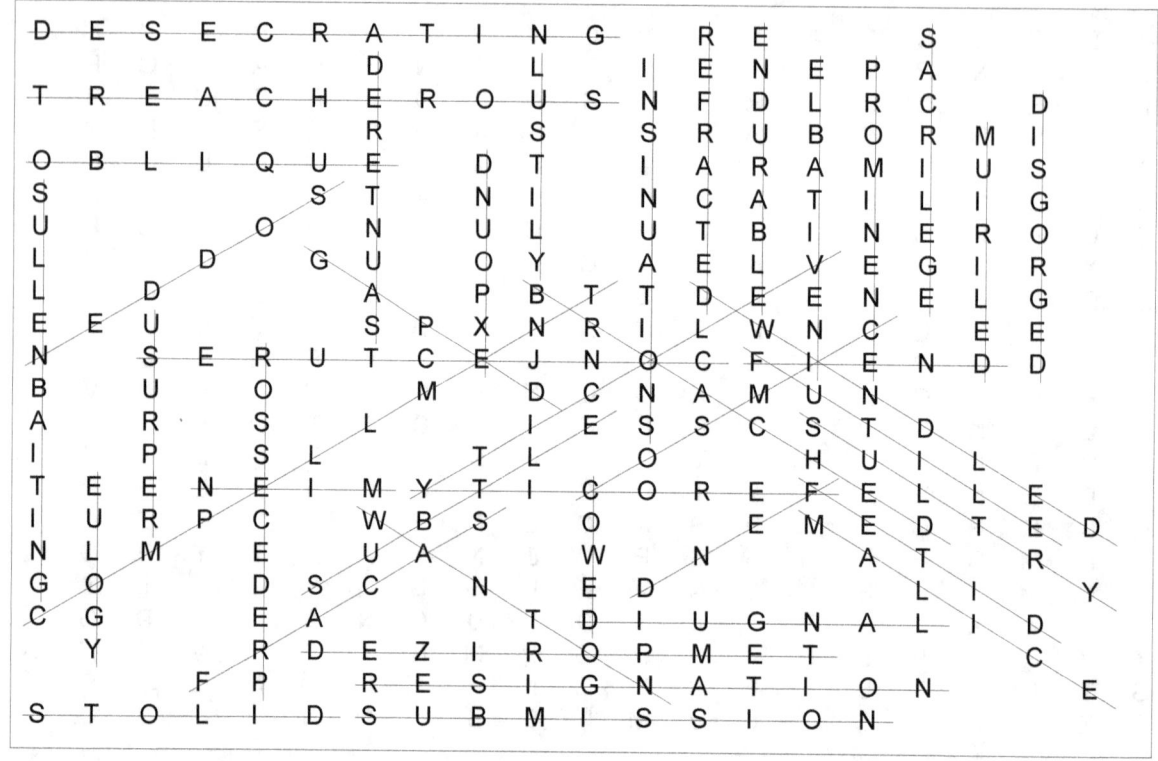

BAITING	DWINDLED	FUTILE	PREDECESSOR	SUBTLE
BROACHED	ENDURABLE	GAPED	PROMINENCE	SULLEN
COMPELLMENT	EULOGY	INEVITABLE	REFRACTED	SULTRY
CONJECTURES	EXPOUND	INSINUATIONS	RESIGNATION	TEMPORIZED
COSMIC	FEND	LANGUID	SACRILEGE	TREACHEROUS
COWED	FEROCITY	LUSTILY	SAUNTERED	USURPER
DELIRIUM	FETID	MALICE	SODDEN	VELOCITY
DESECRATING	FIEND	MIEN	STOLID	WANTON
DISGORGED	FRACAS	OBLIQUE	SUBMISSION	

Their Eyes Were Watching God Vocabulary Word Search 4

Words are placed backwards, forward, diagonally, up and down. Words listed below are included in the maze. Circle the hidden vocabulary words in the maze.

```
T R E A C H E R O U S U R P E R L E K W
Y E K G A L L A N T L Y O D G S U U S S
X H M T R I W B H J M S W E U S L C Z
T Y S P N Q T G W B A Y S I L L T O D Q
N P Y B O E U Q I L B O E N I T I G R W
D O N R I R F C I H W K C D R R L Y K D
D C O O S Y I C N N Z M E L C Y Y S L W
I R I A S F E E S D U D E A J U E A R
S I T C I R P L E E F I E D S O B X C W
E T A H M K T F T D Z R R D L L A C E S
N E N E B B V C W C V I P U M S I R R S
G S G D U G A Z A L S L D M T A T U A K
A B I S S R F D N Z J E F J G U I C T C
G T S Y F D I Q T V R D E B M N N I I J
E F E E R P E L O C V N N W N T G A N G
D P R O M I N E N C E Y D I T E F T G S
X W S A H G D I I D S I E N X R P I A J
H W U L C G Z M D L U T W P R E R N P N
D V L K G A S O Z G T C O S J D D G E N
Z M L F R O S R N R M U C L V Q Z I D G
M N E Y C Q N A J P N B G T I D M Z G Y
H N N C R J L K Q D S C C K M D N T F T
```

BAITING	EXPOUND	INCREDULOUS	REFRACTED	SULTRY
BROACHED	FEND	LACERATING	RESIGNATION	TEMPORIZED
COSMIC	FETID	LANGUID	SACRILEGE	TREACHEROUS
COWED	FIEND	LUSTILY	SAUNTERED	USURPER
DELIRIUM	FRACAS	MALICE	SODDEN	WANTON
DISENGAGED	FUTILE	MIEN	STOLID	
DWINDLED	GALLANTLY	OBLIQUE	SUBMISSION	
EULOGY	GAPED	PREDECESSOR	SUBTLE	
EXCRUCIATING	HYPOCRITES	PROMINENCE	SULLEN	

Their Eyes Were Watching God Vocabulary Word Search 4 Answer Key

Words are placed backwards, forward, diagonally, up and down. Words listed below are included in the maze. Circle the hidden vocabulary words in the maze.

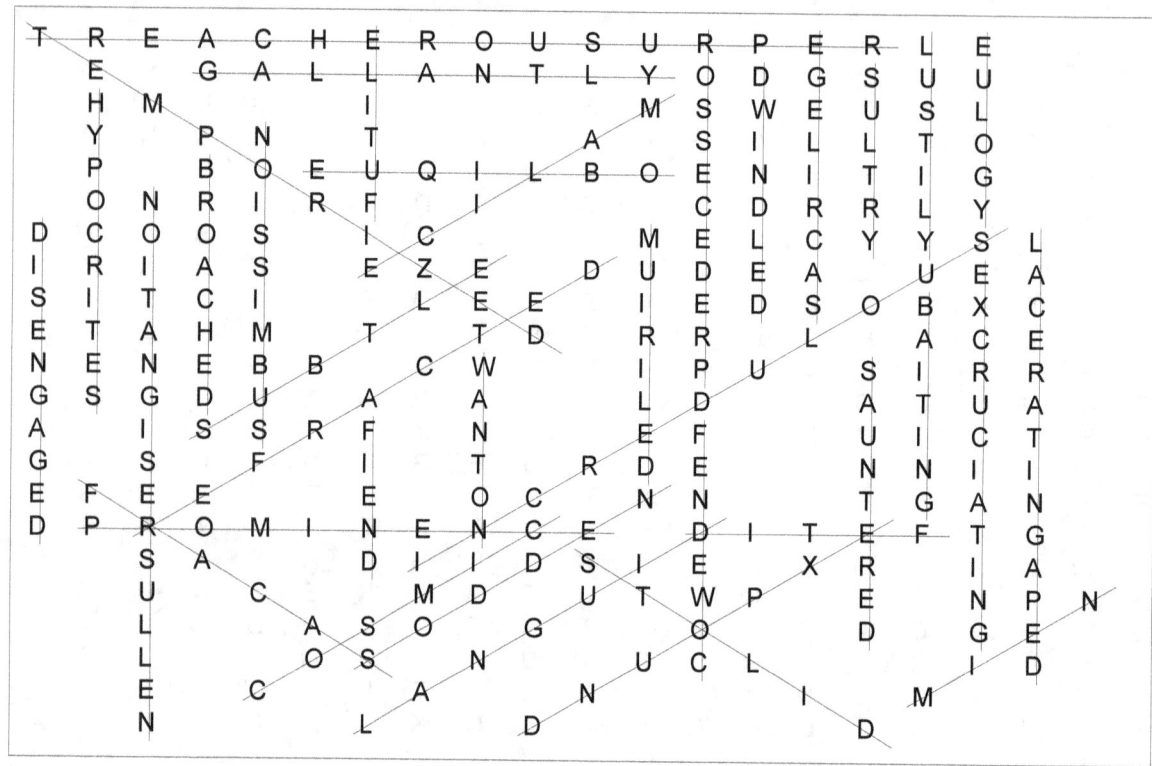

BAITING	EXPOUND	INCREDULOUS	REFRACTED	SULTRY
BROACHED	FEND	LACERATING	RESIGNATION	TEMPORIZED
COSMIC	FETID	LANGUID	SACRILEGE	TREACHEROUS
COWED	FIEND	LUSTILY	SAUNTERED	USURPER
DELIRIUM	FRACAS	MALICE	SODDEN	WANTON
DISENGAGED	FUTILE	MIEN	STOLID	
DWINDLED	GALLANTLY	OBLIQUE	SUBMISSION	
EULOGY	GAPED	PREDECESSOR	SUBTLE	
EXCRUCIATING	HYPOCRITES	PROMINENCE	SULLEN	

Their Eyes Were Watching God Vocabulary Crossword 1

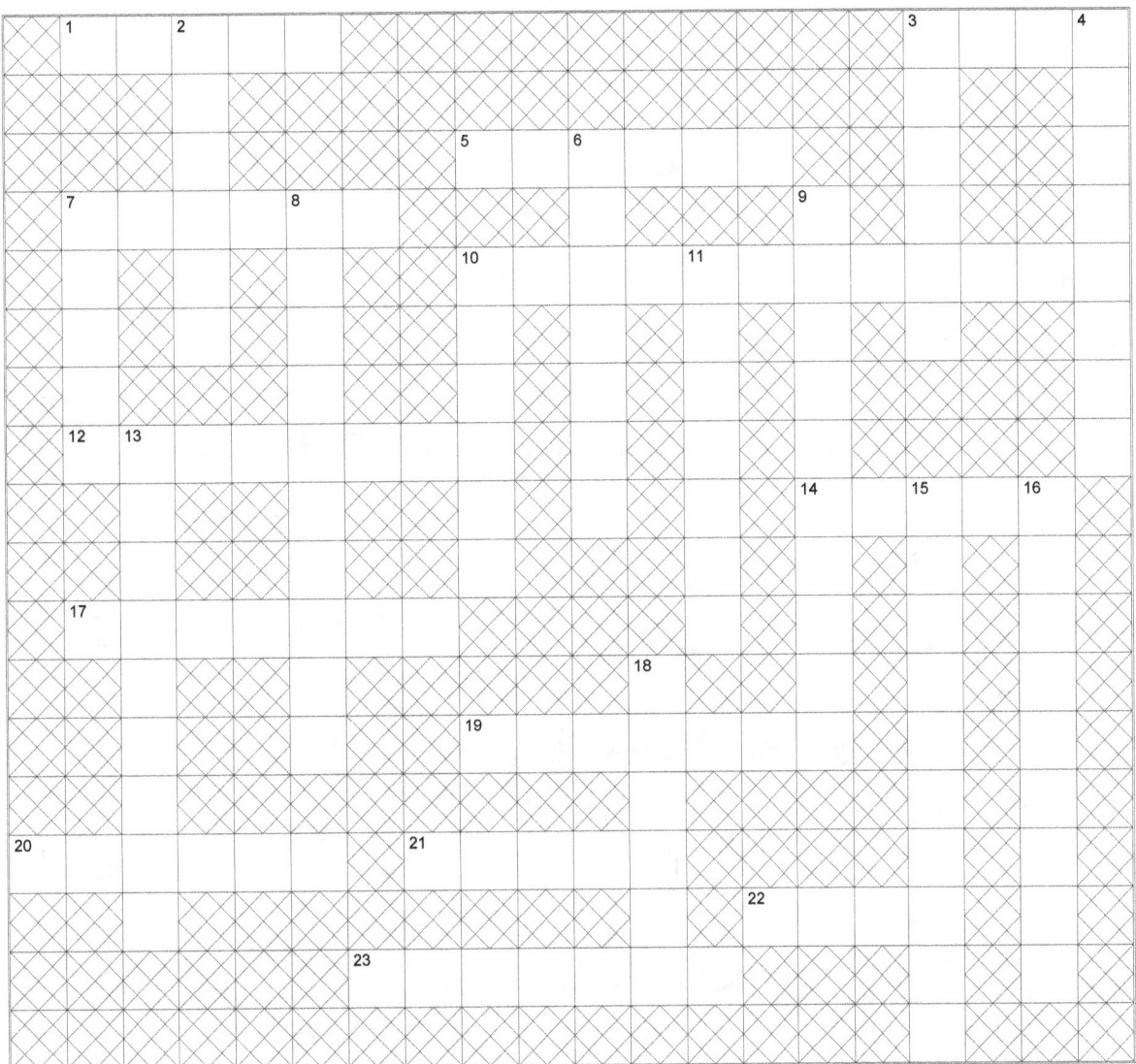

Across
1. Bullied
3. Resist; push away
5. Speech or praise about a dead person
7. Having no useful result
10. United into one system; combined
12. Mental confusion caused by illness
14. Opened wide
17. Robustly; strongly
19. Explain; give a detailed account
20. Sulky; morose
21. Bad or evil person
22. Manner or appearance
23. Taunting, teasing, luring

Down
2. Cruel; merciless
3. A fight; a brawl
4. Became gradually smaller until nothing remained
6. Lacking energy or vitality; weak
7. Having an offensive odor
8. Ripping; cutting; tearing
9. Released; detached
10. Universal; vast
11. Slanted
13. Able to be tolerated for a long time
15. Widely known; being easily identified
16. Vomited; threw up
18. Soaked; saturated

Their Eyes Were Watching God Vocabulary Crossword 1 Answer Key

```
 1C  2W  E  D              3F  E  N  4D
     A                      R        W
     N        5E  6L  O  G  Y  A     I
 7F  U  8T  I  L  E     A     9D  C  N
 E   O   A     10C  O  N  11S  O  L  I  D  A  T  E  D
 T   N   C     O     G   B    S     S           L
 I       E     S     U   L    E                 E
 12D 13E L  I  R  I  U  M  I     I              N              D
     N      A     I     D  Q    14G 15A P  16E
     D      T     C        U    A   R     I
 17L U  S  T  I  L  Y      E    G   O     S
     R      N              18S      E  M  G
     A      G      19E X  P  O  U  N  D  I  O
     B                     D           N  R
 20S U  L  L  E  N  21F I  E  N  D         E  G
     E                     E    22M I  E  N  E
            23B A  I  T  I  N  G       C     D
                                              E
```

Across
1. Bullied
3. Resist; push away
5. Speech or praise about a dead person
7. Having no useful result
10. United into one system; combined
12. Mental confusion caused by illness
14. Opened wide
17. Robustly; strongly
19. Explain; give a detailed account
20. Sulky; morose
21. Bad or evil person
22. Manner or appearance
23. Taunting, teasing, luring

Down
2. Cruel; merciless
3. A fight; a brawl
4. Became gradually smaller until nothing remained
6. Lacking energy or vitality; weak
7. Having an offensive odor
8. Ripping; cutting; tearing
9. Released; detached
10. Universal; vast
11. Slanted
13. Able to be tolerated for a long time
15. Widely known; being easily identified
16. Vomited; threw up
18. Soaked; saturated

Their Eyes Were Watching God Vocabulary Crossword 2

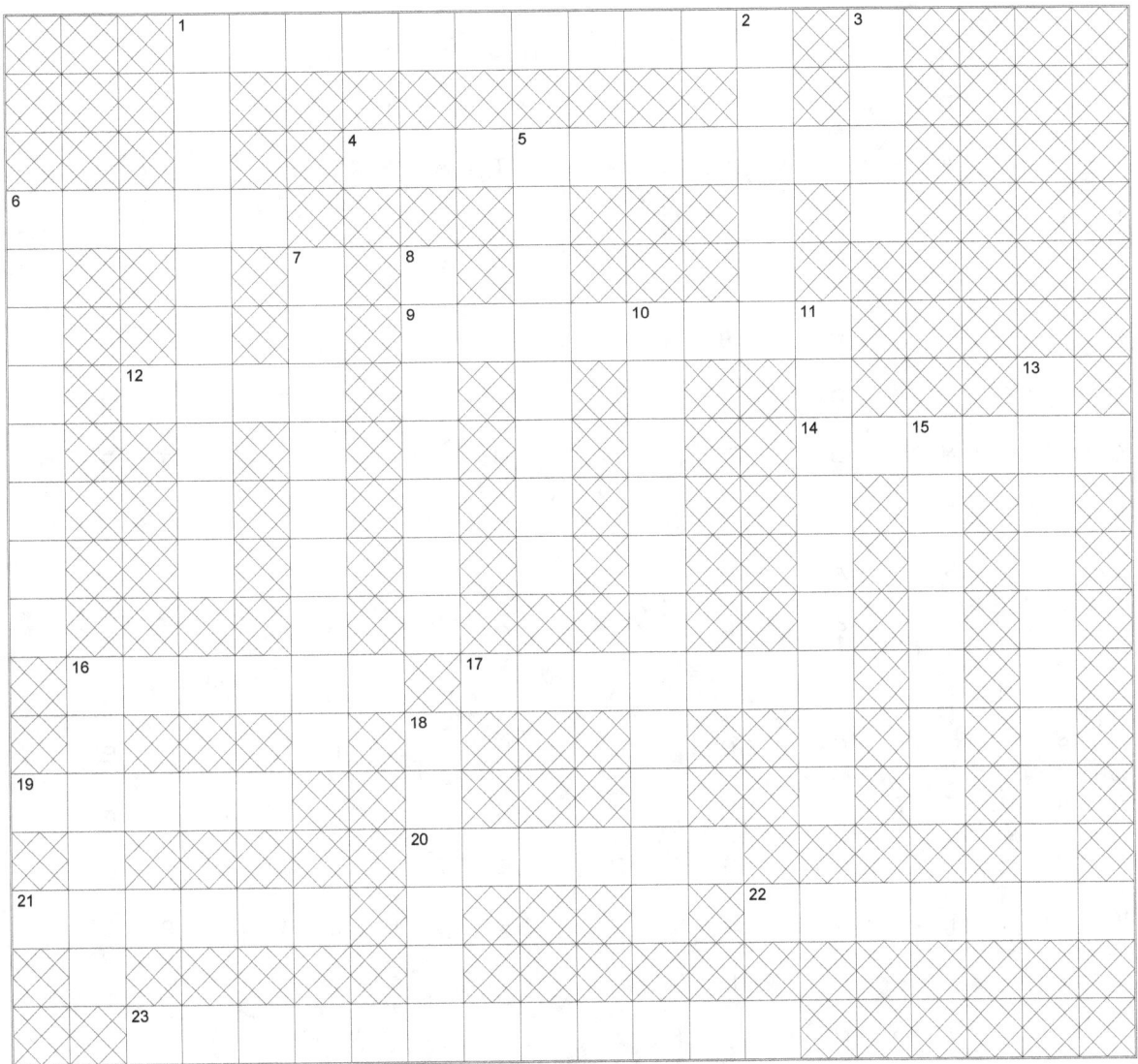

Across
1. Dangerous
4. Unavoidable
6. Bad or evil person
9. Brought up for discussion
12. Resist; push away
14. Very hot and humid
16. Having no useful result
17. Taunting, teasing, luring
19. Opened wide
20. Soaked; saturated
21. Cruel; merciless
22. One who grabs money or property
23. Intensely painful; agonizing

Down
1. People without permanent homes
2. Difficult to detect
3. Manner or appearance
5. Speed
6. Savageness; fierceness
7. Able to be tolerated for a long time
8. Slanted
10. Ideas formed from guessing
11. Vomited; threw up
13. Widely known; being easily identified
15. Lacking energy or vitality; weak
16. A fight; a brawl
18. Universal; vast

Their Eyes Were Watching God Vocabulary Crossword 2 Answer Key

Across
1. Dangerous
4. Unavoidable
6. Bad or evil person
9. Brought up for discussion
12. Resist; push away
14. Very hot and humid
16. Having no useful result
17. Taunting, teasing, luring
19. Opened wide
20. Soaked; saturated
21. Cruel; merciless
22. One who grabs money or property
23. Intensely painful; agonizing

Down
1. People without permanent homes
2. Difficult to detect
3. Manner or appearance
5. Speed
6. Savageness; fierceness
7. Able to be tolerated for a long time
8. Slanted
10. Ideas formed from guessing
11. Vomited; threw up
13. Widely known; being easily identified
15. Lacking energy or vitality; weak
16. A fight; a brawl
18. Universal; vast

Their Eyes Were Watching God Vocabulary Crossword 3

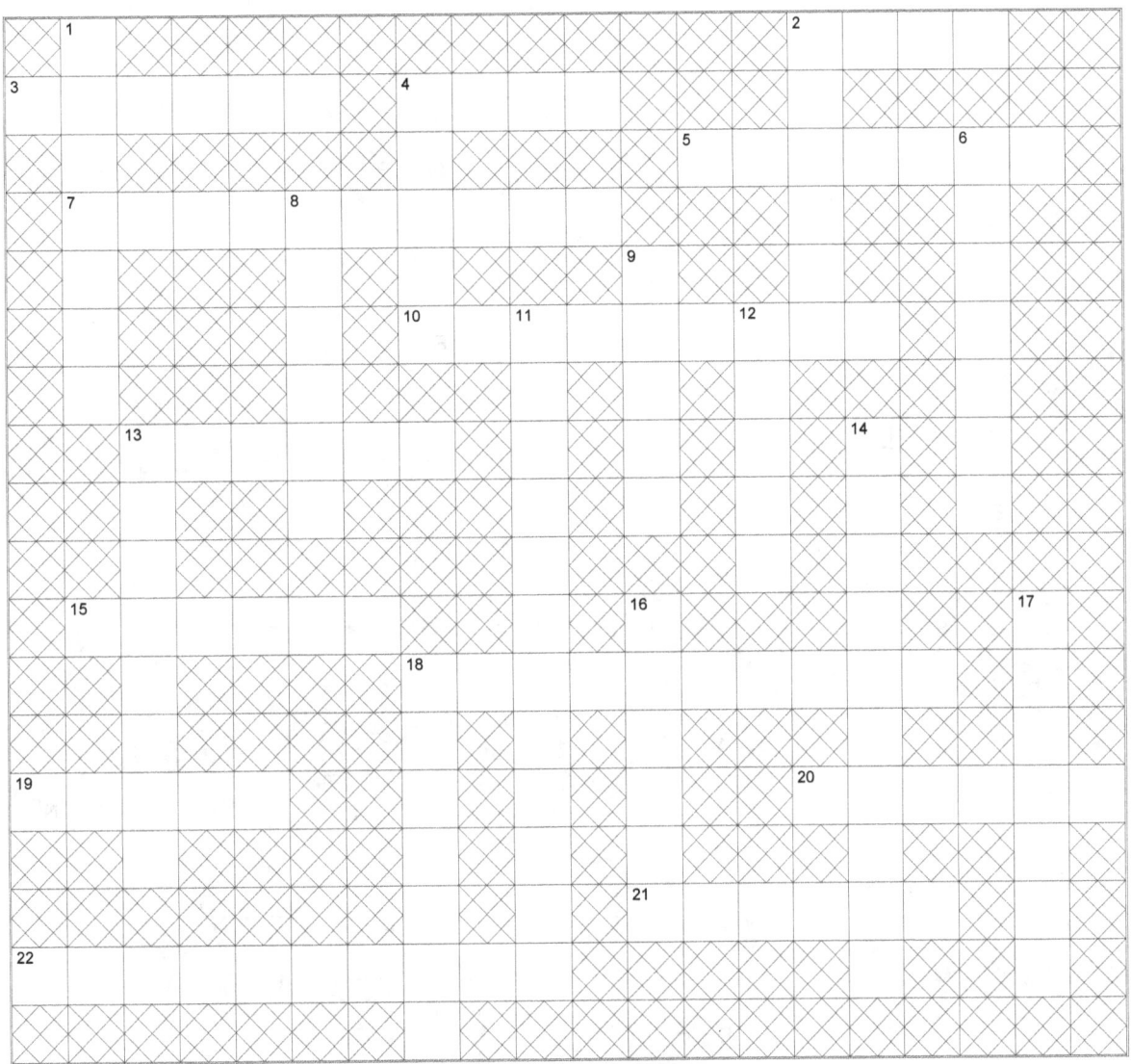

Across
2. Manner or appearance
3. Very hot and humid
4. Resist; push away
5. Slanted
7. People without permanent homes
10. Vomited; threw up
13. Having no useful result
15. Universal; vast
18. Ripping; cutting; tearing
19. Having an offensive odor
20. Cruel; merciless
21. Sulky; morose
22. Giving in to another

Down
1. Robustly; strongly
2. Extreme ill-will or spite
4. Bad or evil person
6. One who grabs money or property
8. Having little or no emotion
9. Bullied
11. Plea; earnest request
12. Opened wide
13. Savageness; fierceness
14. Released; detached
16. A fight; a brawl
17. Explain; give a detailed account
18. Lacking energy or vitality; weak

Their Eyes Were Watching God Vocabulary Crossword 3 Answer Key

Across
2. Manner or appearance
3. Very hot and humid
4. Resist; push away
5. Slanted
7. People without permanent homes
10. Vomited; threw up
13. Having no useful result
15. Universal; vast
18. Ripping; cutting; tearing
19. Having an offensive odor
20. Cruel; merciless
21. Sulky; morose
22. Giving in to another

Down
1. Robustly; strongly
2. Extreme ill-will or spite
4. Bad or evil person
6. One who grabs money or property
8. Having little or no emotion
9. Bullied
11. Plea; earnest request
12. Opened wide
13. Savageness; fierceness
14. Released; detached
16. A fight; a brawl
17. Explain; give a detailed account
18. Lacking energy or vitality; weak

Their Eyes Were Watching God Vocabulary Crossword 4

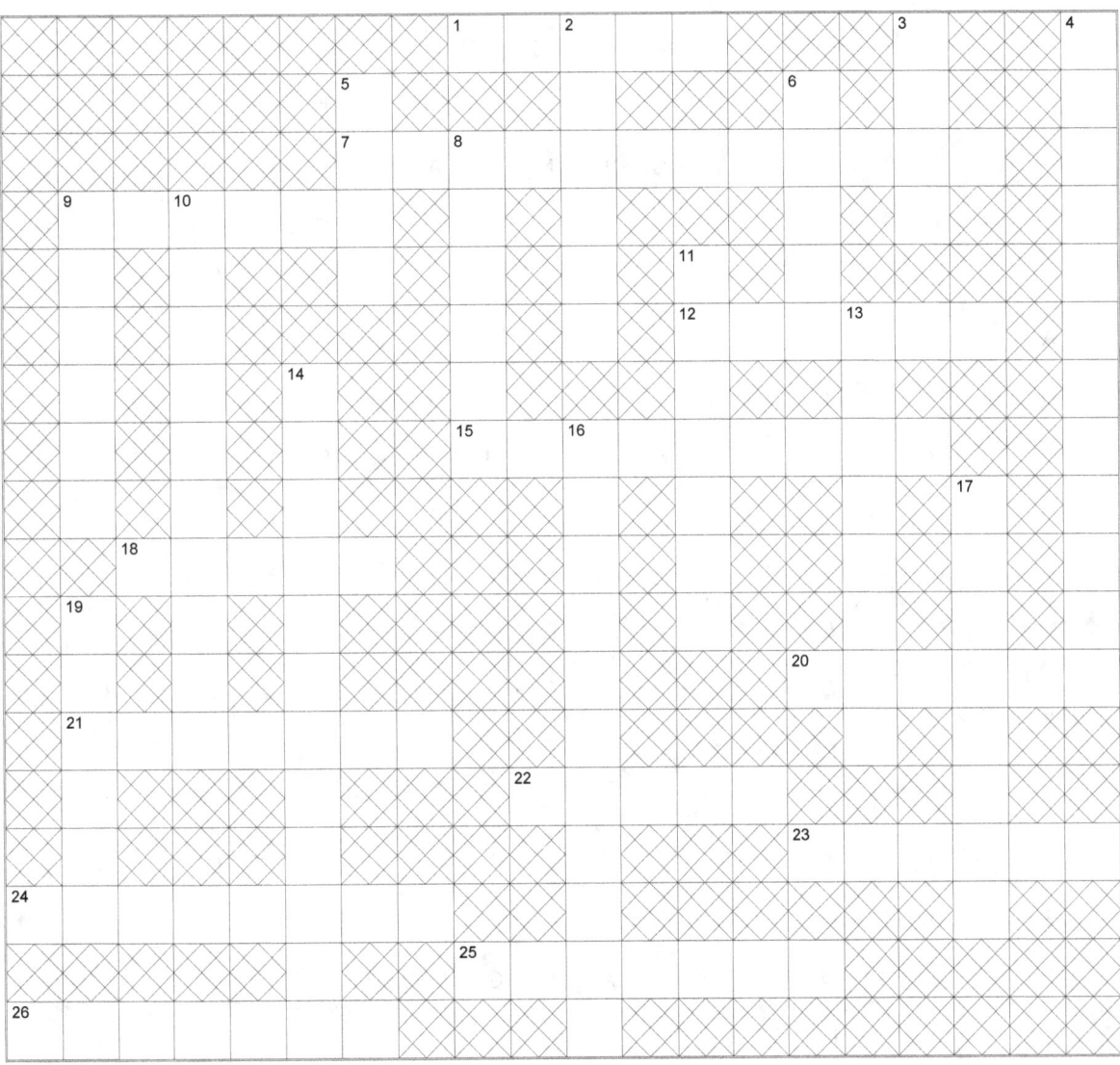

Across
1. Bullied
7. Subtly made suggestions
9. Having no useful result
12. Soaked; saturated
15. Able to be tolerated for a long time
18. Having an offensive odor
20. Speech or praise about a dead person
21. Robustly; strongly
22. Opened wide
23. Very hot and humid
24. Speed
25. Lacking energy or vitality; weak
26. Explain; give a detailed account

Down
2. Cruel; merciless
3. Resist; push away
4. Combative in nature; belligerently; rebelliously
5. Manner or appearance
6. Bad or evil person
8. Difficult to detect
9. A fight; a brawl
10. People without permanent homes
11. One who grabs money or property
13. Mental confusion caused by illness
14. Area of control or power
16. Violating the sacredness of
17. Savageness; fierceness
19. Extreme ill-will or spite

Their Eyes Were Watching God Vocabulary Crossword 4 Answer Key

Across
1. Bullied
7. Subtly made suggestions
9. Having no useful result
12. Soaked; saturated
15. Able to be tolerated for a long time
18. Having an offensive odor
20. Speech or praise about a dead person
21. Robustly; strongly
22. Opened wide
23. Very hot and humid
24. Speed
25. Lacking energy or vitality; weak
26. Explain; give a detailed account

Down
2. Cruel; merciless
3. Resist; push away
4. Combative in nature; belligerently; rebelliously
5. Manner or appearance
6. Bad or evil person
8. Difficult to detect
9. A fight; a brawl
10. People without permanent homes
11. One who grabs money or property
13. Mental confusion caused by illness
14. Area of control or power
16. Violating the sacredness of
17. Savageness; fierceness
19. Extreme ill-will or spite

Their Eyes Were Watching God Vocabulary Juggle Letters 1

1. LUNSEL = 1. _____
   Sulky; morose

2. RDOAEBHC = 2. _____
   Brought up for discussion

3. UEIRINTCACGX = 3. _____
   Intensely painful; agonizing

4. TINIIONASSNU = 4. _____
   Subtly made suggestions

5. CTEUJOSCNER = 5. _____
   Ideas formed from guessing

6. ERRFTECAD = 6. _____
   Deflected from a straight path

7. TDIOLS = 7. _____
   Having little or no emotion

8. DEIMRILU = 8. _____
   Mental confusion caused by illness

9. UYEGLO = 9. _____
   Speech or praise about a dead person

10. NSSUIISMBO =10. _____
    Giving in to another

11. OFETICRY =11. _____
    Savageness; fierceness

12. ARCASF =12. _____
    A fight; a brawl

13. EONCRIMNPE =13. _____
    Widely known; being easily identified

14. LBEDRNEAU =14. _____
    Able to be tolerated for a long time

15. IRGDGDSEO =15. _____
    Vomited; threw up

Their Eyes Were Watching God Vocabulary Juggle Letters 1 Answer Key

1. LUNSEL = 1. SULLEN
   Sulky; morose

2. RDOAEBHC = 2. BROACHED
   Brought up for discussion

3. UEIRINTCACGX = 3. EXCRUCIATING
   Intensely painful; agonizing

4. TINIIONASSNU = 4. INSINUATIONS
   Subtly made suggestions

5. CTEUJOSCNER = 5. CONJECTURES
   Ideas formed from guessing

6. ERRFTECAD = 6. REFRACTED
   Deflected from a straight path

7. TDIOLS = 7. STOLID
   Having little or no emotion

8. DEIMRILU = 8. DELIRIUM
   Mental confusion caused by illness

9. UYEGLO = 9. EULOGY
   Speech or praise about a dead person

10. NSSUIISMBO = 10. SUBMISSION
    Giving in to another

11. OFETICRY = 11. FEROCITY
    Savageness; fierceness

12. ARCASF = 12. FRACAS
    A fight; a brawl

13. EONCRIMNPE = 13. PROMINENCE
    Widely known; being easily identified

14. LBEDRNEAU = 14. ENDURABLE
    Able to be tolerated for a long time

15. IRGDGDSEO = 15. DISGORGED
    Vomited; threw up

Their Eyes Were Watching God Vocabulary Juggle Letters 2

1. NTSEECCRUJO = 1. _____
   Ideas formed from guessing

2. REORUCHTASE = 2. _____
   Dangerous

3. CTSUIRNDJIIO = 3. _____
   Area of control or power

4. ASLCIEREG = 4. _____
   Against something sacred

5. EULDSIRCUON = 5. _____
   Unbelieving; skeptical

6. TAESDECIRNG = 6. _____
   Violating the sacredness of

7. OATTNPRSRGI = 7. _____
   Bowing down in adoration or submission

8. TELUIF = 8. _____
   Having no useful result

9. ERFDETRCA = 9. _____
   Deflected from a straight path

10. COSIMC = 10. _____
    Universal; vast

11. IPOERDTZME = 11. _____
    Negotiated to gain time

12. NGIAIECXUCRT = 12. _____
    Intensely painful; agonizing

13. OSDEDN = 13. _____
    Soaked; saturated

14. NINISOTSUAIN = 14. _____
    Subtly made suggestions

15. DSIOLT = 15. _____
    Having little or no emotion

Their Eyes Were Watching God Vocabulary Juggle Letters 2 Answer Key

1. NTSEECCRUJO = 1. CONJECTURES
   Ideas formed from guessing

2. REORUCHTASE = 2. TREACHEROUS
   Dangerous

3. CTSUIRNDJIIO = 3. JURISDICTION
   Area of control or power

4. ASLCIEREG = 4. SACRILEGE
   Against something sacred

5. EULDSIRCUON = 5. INCREDULOUS
   Unbelieving; skeptical

6. TAESDECIRNG = 6. DESECRATING
   Violating the sacredness of

7. OATTNPRSRGI = 7. PROSTRATING
   Bowing down in adoration or submission

8. TELUIF = 8. FUTILE
   Having no useful result

9. ERFDETRCA = 9. REFRACTED
   Deflected from a straight path

10. COSIMC = 10. COSMIC
    Universal; vast

11. IPOERDTZME = 11. TEMPORIZED
    Negotiated to gain time

12. NGIAIECXUCRT = 12. EXCRUCIATING
    Intensely painful; agonizing

13. OSDEDN = 13. SODDEN
    Soaked; saturated

14. NINISOTSUAIN = 14. INSINUATIONS
    Subtly made suggestions

15. DSIOLT = 15. STOLID
    Having little or no emotion

Their Eyes Were Watching God Vocabulary Juggle Letters 3

1. EDCOW = 1. _____
　　　　　　　　Bullied

2. OSMCIC = 2. _____
　　　　　　　　Universal; vast

3. RSELACEGI = 3. _____
　　　　　　　　Against something sacred

4. DNDILEWD = 4. _____
　　　　　　　　Became gradually smaller until nothing remained

5. NWNTAO = 5. _____
　　　　　　　　Cruel; merciless

6. NOGRSTPIRTA = 6. _____
　　　　　　　　Bowing down in adoration or submission

7. GUALDNI = 7. _____
　　　　　　　　Lacking energy or vitality; weak

8. YIORFTEC = 8. _____
　　　　　　　　Savageness; fierceness

9. GULYOE = 9. _____
　　　　　　　　Speech or praise about a dead person

10. ECJENCOSUTR =10. _____
　　　　　　　　Ideas formed from guessing

11. HORCADBE =11. _____
　　　　　　　　Brought up for discussion

12. LLUENS =12. _____
　　　　　　　　Sulky; morose

13. NEDF =13. _____
　　　　　　　　Resist; push away

14. IOEGGSRDD =14. _____
　　　　　　　　Vomited; threw up

15. EDINF =15. _____
　　　　　　　　Bad or evil person

Their Eyes Were Watching God Vocabulary Juggle Letters 3 Answer Key

1. EDCOW = 1. COWED
   Bullied

2. OSMCIC = 2. COSMIC
   Universal; vast

3. RSELACEGI = 3. SACRILEGE
   Against something sacred

4. DNDILEWD = 4. DWINDLED
   Became gradually smaller until nothing remained

5. NWNTAO = 5. WANTON
   Cruel; merciless

6. NOGRSTPIRTA = 6. PROSTRATING
   Bowing down in adoration or submission

7. GUALDNI = 7. LANGUID
   Lacking energy or vitality; weak

8. YIORFTEC = 8. FEROCITY
   Savageness; fierceness

9. GULYOE = 9. EULOGY
   Speech or praise about a dead person

10. ECJENCOSUTR = 10. CONJECTURES
    Ideas formed from guessing

11. HORCADBE = 11. BROACHED
    Brought up for discussion

12. LLUENS = 12. SULLEN
    Sulky; morose

13. NEDF = 13. FEND
    Resist; push away

14. IOEGGSRDD = 14. DISGORGED
    Vomited; threw up

15. EDINF = 15. FIEND
    Bad or evil person

Their Eyes Were Watching God Vocabulary Juggle Letters 4

1. ECMLAI = 1. _____
   Extreme ill-will or spite

2. ORSESDEPCER = 2. _____
   An ancestor; one who came before

3. IQEUBLO = 3. _____
   Slanted

4. TSELUB = 4. _____
   Difficult to detect

5. YLTURS = 5. _____
   Very hot and humid

6. CEHOIPTSRY = 6. _____
   People who say one thing but do the opposite

7. NEULBEDRA = 7. _____
   Able to be tolerated for a long time

8. MPLELTECMNO = 8. _____
   Strong urging forces

9. DGNAILU = 9. _____
   Lacking energy or vitality; weak

10. NUESLL = 10. _____
    Sulky; morose

11. AESGRLCEI = 11. _____
    Against something sacred

12. GNIETRCIACUX = 12. _____
    Intensely painful; agonizing

13. IPRGOASRTNT = 13. _____
    Bowing down in adoration or submission

14. CREAETDFR = 14. _____
    Deflected from a straight path

15. ECWOD = 15. _____
    Bullied

Their Eyes Were Watching God Vocabulary Juggle Letters 4 Answer Key

1. ECMLAI = 1. MALICE
   Extreme ill-will or spite

2. ORSESDEPCER = 2. PREDECESSOR
   An ancestor; one who came before

3. IQEUBLO = 3. OBLIQUE
   Slanted

4. TSELUB = 4. SUBTLE
   Difficult to detect

5. YLTURS = 5. SULTRY
   Very hot and humid

6. CEHOIPTSRY = 6. HYPOCRITES
   People who say one thing but do the opposite

7. NEULBEDRA = 7. ENDURABLE
   Able to be tolerated for a long time

8. MPLELTECMNO = 8. COMPELLMENT
   Strong urging forces

9. DGNAILU = 9. LANGUID
   Lacking energy or vitality; weak

10. NUESLL = 10. SULLEN
    Sulky; morose

11. AESGRLCEI = 11. SACRILEGE
    Against something sacred

12. GNIETRCIACUX = 12. EXCRUCIATING
    Intensely painful; agonizing

13. IPRGOASRTNT = 13. PROSTRATING
    Bowing down in adoration or submission

14. CREAETDFR = 14. REFRACTED
    Deflected from a straight path

15. ECWOD = 15. COWED
    Bullied

BAITING	Taunting, teasing, luring
BROACHED	Brought up for discussion
COMPELLMENT	Strong urging forces
CONJECTURES	Ideas formed from guessing
CONSOLIDATED	United into one system; combined
COSMIC	Universal; vast

COWED	Bullied
DELIRIUM	Mental confusion caused by illness
DESECRATING	Violating the sacredness of
DISENGAGED	Released; detached
DISGORGED	Vomited; threw up
DWINDLED	Became gradually smaller until nothing remained

ENDURABLE	Able to be tolerated for a long time
EULOGY	Speech or praise about a dead person
EXCRUCIATING	Intensely painful; agonizing
EXPOUND	Explain; give a detailed account
FEND	Resist; push away
FEROCITY	Savageness; fierceness

FETID	Having an offensive odor
FIEND	Bad or evil person
FRACAS	A fight; a brawl
FUTILE	Having no useful result
GALLANTLY	Nobly; boldy
GAPED	Opened wide

HYPOCRITES	People who say one thing but do the opposite
INCREDULOUS	Unbelieving; skeptical
INEVITABLE	Unavoidable
INSINUATIONS	Subtly made suggestions
JURISDICTION	Area of control or power
LACERATING	Ripping; cutting; tearing

LANGUID	Lacking energy or vitality; weak
LANGUISHED	Wasted away; weakened
LUSTILY	Robustly; strongly
MALICE	Extreme ill-will or spite
MIEN	Manner or appearance
OBLIQUE	Slanted

PERSEVERANCE	Persistence; dogged trying
PREDECESSOR	An ancestor; one who came before
PROMINENCE	Widely known; being easily identified
PROSTRATING	Bowing down in adoration or submission
PUGNACIOUSLY	Combative in nature; belligerently; rebelliously
REFRACTED	Deflected from a straight path

RESIGNATION	Unresisting acceptance
SACRILEGE	Against something sacred
SAUNTERED	Strolled
SODDEN	Soaked; saturated
STOLID	Having little or no emotion
SUBMISSION	Giving in to another

SUBTLE	Difficult to detect
SULLEN	Sulky; morose
SULTRY	Very hot and humid
SUPPLICATION	Plea; earnest request
TEMPORIZED	Negotiated to gain time
TRANSIENTS	People without permanent homes

TREACHEROUS	Dangerous
USURPER	One who grabs money or property
VELOCITY	Speed
WANTON	Cruel; merciless

Their Eyes Were Watching God V

SAUNTERED	ENDURABLE	FIEND	CONSOLIDATED	PROMINENCE
INSINUATIONS	COMPELLMENT	STOLID	FEROCITY	LANGUISHED
SULTRY	EXPOUND	FREE SPACE	FEND	TEMPORIZED
PERSEVERANCE	SODDEN	FRACAS	DELIRIUM	TREACHEROUS
LUSTILY	DWINDLED	OBLIQUE	PUGNACIOUSLY	DISENGAGED

Their Eyes Were Watching God V

SACRILEGE	EXCRUCIATING	PROSTRATING	TRANSIENTS	HYPOCRITES
CONJECTURES	BROACHED	FETID	WANTON	EULOGY
LACERATING	SUBTLE	FREE SPACE	INCREDULOUS	SUPPLICATION
MIEN	REFRACTED	GALLANTLY	MALICE	SUBMISSION
RESIGNATION	DISGORGED	DESECRATING	USURPER	LANGUID

Their Eyes Were Watching God V

TEMPORIZED	BROACHED	RESIGNATION	SACRILEGE	INCREDULOUS
LACERATING	LANGUID	DELIRIUM	FIEND	COWED
SUPPLICATION	PUGNACIOUSLY	FREE SPACE	CONJECTURES	COMPELLMENT
HYPOCRITES	VELOCITY	MIEN	INEVITABLE	SUBMISSION
PERSEVERANCE	EXCRUCIATING	SODDEN	REFRACTED	SAUNTERED

Their Eyes Were Watching God V

ENDURABLE	USURPER	STOLID	DWINDLED	SULLEN
EULOGY	EXPOUND	CONSOLIDATED	GAPED	PREDECESSOR
JURISDICTION	WANTON	FREE SPACE	LANGUISHED	FRACAS
FETID	FEND	SUBTLE	TREACHEROUS	OBLIQUE
FUTILE	DESECRATING	LUSTILY	GALLANTLY	DISGORGED

Their Eyes Were Watching God V

WANTON	DISENGAGED	BAITING	LANGUID	HYPOCRITES
SULLEN	JURISDICTION	PROSTRATING	INCREDULOUS	PERSEVERANCE
BROACHED	FUTILE	FREE SPACE	CONSOLIDATED	COMPELLMENT
RESIGNATION	ENDURABLE	PREDECESSOR	FEND	CONJECTURES
TEMPORIZED	SUPPLICATION	SACRILEGE	GALLANTLY	DELIRIUM

Their Eyes Were Watching God V

EXPOUND	COSMIC	SAUNTERED	STOLID	DISGORGED
OBLIQUE	FIEND	MIEN	DESECRATING	INSINUATIONS
EULOGY	EXCRUCIATING	FREE SPACE	SUBTLE	TRANSIENTS
USURPER	SODDEN	SULTRY	INEVITABLE	COWED
LUSTILY	PROMINENCE	DWINDLED	LANGUISHED	FEROCITY

Their Eyes Were Watching God V

INEVITABLE	SUPPLICATION	LACERATING	TEMPORIZED	SUBTLE
GALLANTLY	INCREDULOUS	CONSOLIDATED	TREACHEROUS	WANTON
SODDEN	INSINUATIONS	FREE SPACE	VELOCITY	FIEND
MIEN	FEROCITY	DISENGAGED	SACRILEGE	BAITING
RESIGNATION	TRANSIENTS	LUSTILY	SULTRY	BROACHED

Their Eyes Were Watching God V

GAPED	EXPOUND	OBLIQUE	DWINDLED	REFRACTED
FEND	PROSTRATING	COWED	FETID	SUBMISSION
FUTILE	EULOGY	FREE SPACE	PROMINENCE	STOLID
DELIRIUM	JURISDICTION	LANGUISHED	COSMIC	CONJECTURES
DESECRATING	USURPER	EXCRUCIATING	SULLEN	DISGORGED

Their Eyes Were Watching God V

FEROCITY	OBLIQUE	COWED	MIEN	FIEND
CONSOLIDATED	TEMPORIZED	DELIRIUM	HYPOCRITES	COMPELLMENT
SACRILEGE	SAUNTERED	FREE SPACE	PREDECESSOR	TREACHEROUS
INSINUATIONS	SULTRY	STOLID	TRANSIENTS	PROSTRATING
EXCRUCIATING	VELOCITY	DESECRATING	COSMIC	GALLANTLY

Their Eyes Were Watching God V

GAPED	DISENGAGED	INCREDULOUS	ENDURABLE	LUSTILY
BAITING	EXPOUND	LANGUISHED	WANTON	EULOGY
SUPPLICATION	RESIGNATION	FREE SPACE	DISGORGED	FUTILE
DWINDLED	SODDEN	SUBMISSION	REFRACTED	MALICE
FEND	PERSEVERANCE	LACERATING	SULLEN	SUBTLE

Their Eyes Were Watching God V

PROMINENCE	SODDEN	COWED	USURPER	JURISDICTION
EXCRUCIATING	RESIGNATION	COMPELLMENT	DWINDLED	DESECRATING
SAUNTERED	PROSTRATING	FREE SPACE	REFRACTED	FUTILE
EULOGY	BAITING	SUBTLE	CONSOLIDATED	TEMPORIZED
MIEN	LANGUID	BROACHED	FEROCITY	DISENGAGED

Their Eyes Were Watching God V

DELIRIUM	VELOCITY	LUSTILY	SULTRY	LACERATING
TREACHEROUS	WANTON	PUGNACIOUSLY	FIEND	MALICE
HYPOCRITES	FETID	FREE SPACE	LANGUISHED	FEND
SUBMISSION	FRACAS	SACRILEGE	TRANSIENTS	INEVITABLE
PREDECESSOR	GALLANTLY	DISGORGED	PERSEVERANCE	STOLID

Their Eyes Were Watching God V

REFRACTED	RESIGNATION	SODDEN	CONSOLIDATED	DISENGAGED
DISGORGED	SACRILEGE	INEVITABLE	GAPED	EXCRUCIATING
DELIRIUM	FRACAS	FREE SPACE	LANGUID	SUBTLE
FIEND	DESECRATING	PROSTRATING	SAUNTERED	COMPELLMENT
TEMPORIZED	ENDURABLE	SULLEN	LANGUISHED	INSINUATIONS

Their Eyes Were Watching God V

COSMIC	TRANSIENTS	USURPER	FUTILE	SULTRY
JURISDICTION	LUSTILY	PUGNACIOUSLY	OBLIQUE	GALLANTLY
BAITING	EXPOUND	FREE SPACE	HYPOCRITES	FETID
SUBMISSION	LACERATING	FEROCITY	DWINDLED	PROMINENCE
VELOCITY	PERSEVERANCE	SUPPLICATION	MIEN	STOLID

Their Eyes Were Watching God V

LANGUID	DISENGAGED	GALLANTLY	SAUNTERED	MIEN
TREACHEROUS	BAITING	RESIGNATION	STOLID	FETID
FEROCITY	PERSEVERANCE	FREE SPACE	PUGNACIOUSLY	FEND
REFRACTED	HYPOCRITES	PROMINENCE	SUBMISSION	OBLIQUE
USURPER	COWED	SULTRY	PREDECESSOR	ENDURABLE

Their Eyes Were Watching God V

DELIRIUM	SULLEN	VELOCITY	INEVITABLE	EXCRUCIATING
WANTON	DISGORGED	SODDEN	COMPELLMENT	SACRILEGE
FUTILE	INCREDULOUS	FREE SPACE	CONJECTURES	MALICE
EXPOUND	TEMPORIZED	BROACHED	LANGUISHED	DWINDLED
CONSOLIDATED	LUSTILY	TRANSIENTS	FRACAS	COSMIC

Their Eyes Were Watching God V

EXPOUND	LANGUID	USURPER	PROMINENCE	DWINDLED
PUGNACIOUSLY	PERSEVERANCE	PROSTRATING	FRACAS	CONSOLIDATED
COSMIC	LANGUISHED	FREE SPACE	VELOCITY	TREACHEROUS
RESIGNATION	FEROCITY	SULLEN	INCREDULOUS	SACRILEGE
EXCRUCIATING	INSINUATIONS	DISENGAGED	SODDEN	MIEN

Their Eyes Were Watching God V

COWED	MALICE	DESECRATING	FIEND	BROACHED
REFRACTED	TRANSIENTS	FUTILE	DELIRIUM	COMPELLMENT
FEND	GAPED	FREE SPACE	INEVITABLE	BAITING
HYPOCRITES	TEMPORIZED	EULOGY	JURISDICTION	CONJECTURES
SUPPLICATION	DISGORGED	PREDECESSOR	GALLANTLY	LACERATING

Their Eyes Were Watching God V

FEND	PERSEVERANCE	SUBMISSION	VELOCITY	SUBTLE
CONJECTURES	PUGNACIOUSLY	TEMPORIZED	JURISDICTION	WANTON
LUSTILY	BROACHED	FREE SPACE	DISENGAGED	ENDURABLE
GALLANTLY	STOLID	COSMIC	SULTRY	BAITING
SACRILEGE	DWINDLED	SUPPLICATION	RESIGNATION	FEROCITY

Their Eyes Were Watching God V

PROMINENCE	FUTILE	TRANSIENTS	COWED	INCREDULOUS
LACERATING	TREACHEROUS	HYPOCRITES	SAUNTERED	PREDECESSOR
FRACAS	GAPED	FREE SPACE	INEVITABLE	COMPELLMENT
SULLEN	USURPER	LANGUID	OBLIQUE	EULOGY
PROSTRATING	EXCRUCIATING	REFRACTED	SODDEN	EXPOUND

Their Eyes Were Watching God V

FIEND	DISENGAGED	COWED	PERSEVERANCE	TREACHEROUS
DELIRIUM	DESECRATING	SUBMISSION	FRACAS	MIEN
PUGNACIOUSLY	LANGUID	FREE SPACE	DWINDLED	EULOGY
EXPOUND	CONSOLIDATED	LACERATING	INSINUATIONS	WANTON
HYPOCRITES	COMPELLMENT	INCREDULOUS	LUSTILY	COSMIC

Their Eyes Were Watching God V

SUPPLICATION	JURISDICTION	PROMINENCE	REFRACTED	MALICE
GAPED	VELOCITY	SUBTLE	FEROCITY	CONJECTURES
SULTRY	EXCRUCIATING	FREE SPACE	FETID	TRANSIENTS
BROACHED	TEMPORIZED	DISGORGED	BAITING	PREDECESSOR
RESIGNATION	SAUNTERED	INEVITABLE	ENDURABLE	USURPER

Their Eyes Were Watching God V

SODDEN	TREACHEROUS	FRACAS	PERSEVERANCE	PREDECESSOR
DISGORGED	COWED	MIEN	FETID	CONSOLIDATED
DELIRIUM	WANTON	FREE SPACE	FIEND	INEVITABLE
SULTRY	SULLEN	ENDURABLE	USURPER	MALICE
BAITING	JURISDICTION	LUSTILY	VELOCITY	EULOGY

Their Eyes Were Watching God V

PROSTRATING	FEROCITY	GALLANTLY	SAUNTERED	HYPOCRITES
TEMPORIZED	DESECRATING	SUBMISSION	REFRACTED	FEND
STOLID	COSMIC	FREE SPACE	INCREDULOUS	EXPOUND
PUGNACIOUSLY	INSINUATIONS	SUPPLICATION	GAPED	LANGUISHED
LACERATING	PROMINENCE	SUBTLE	FUTILE	BROACHED

Their Eyes Were Watching God V

PUGNACIOUSLY	JURISDICTION	WANTON	BROACHED	SULLEN
DESECRATING	DISENGAGED	COMPELLMENT	GAPED	FRACAS
FUTILE	PROMINENCE	FREE SPACE	GALLANTLY	SUPPLICATION
LUSTILY	OBLIQUE	ENDURABLE	HYPOCRITES	SULTRY
PERSEVERANCE	FEND	SUBTLE	PREDECESSOR	BAITING

Their Eyes Were Watching God V

EULOGY	LACERATING	FETID	TEMPORIZED	INCREDULOUS
MALICE	STOLID	REFRACTED	FIEND	COWED
INEVITABLE	SODDEN	FREE SPACE	SACRILEGE	SAUNTERED
LANGUID	LANGUISHED	TRANSIENTS	FEROCITY	DELIRIUM
CONJECTURES	RESIGNATION	DWINDLED	PROSTRATING	EXPOUND

Their Eyes Were Watching God V

EXCRUCIATING	DISGORGED	ENDURABLE	PERSEVERANCE	SAUNTERED
TRANSIENTS	FRACAS	TEMPORIZED	GAPED	DWINDLED
HYPOCRITES	EULOGY	FREE SPACE	PROMINENCE	COWED
PUGNACIOUSLY	GALLANTLY	WANTON	PROSTRATING	SULTRY
VELOCITY	RESIGNATION	SUBMISSION	REFRACTED	LUSTILY

Their Eyes Were Watching God V

EXPOUND	SUBTLE	DISENGAGED	INEVITABLE	LACERATING
FEROCITY	OBLIQUE	FEND	USURPER	STOLID
SULLEN	BAITING	FREE SPACE	FUTILE	MIEN
PREDECESSOR	MALICE	FIEND	SACRILEGE	LANGUISHED
DESECRATING	INSINUATIONS	CONJECTURES	SUPPLICATION	FETID

Their Eyes Were Watching God V

FUTILE	SAUNTERED	CONJECTURES	LACERATING	SULTRY
INEVITABLE	SODDEN	GAPED	LUSTILY	DESECRATING
RESIGNATION	USURPER	FREE SPACE	SUBMISSION	VELOCITY
FETID	OBLIQUE	LANGUID	PROMINENCE	DISGORGED
REFRACTED	TRANSIENTS	ENDURABLE	MALICE	PROSTRATING

Their Eyes Were Watching God V

EXCRUCIATING	DISENGAGED	SUPPLICATION	PREDECESSOR	INCREDULOUS
SULLEN	JURISDICTION	MIEN	EULOGY	DWINDLED
GALLANTLY	STOLID	FREE SPACE	FRACAS	SACRILEGE
PUGNACIOUSLY	COSMIC	EXPOUND	TEMPORIZED	LANGUISHED
DELIRIUM	HYPOCRITES	TREACHEROUS	COWED	BROACHED

Their Eyes Were Watching God V

SULLEN	PROSTRATING	CONJECTURES	CONSOLIDATED	DISENGAGED
PROMINENCE	PUGNACIOUSLY	COWED	LUSTILY	TREACHEROUS
COSMIC	EXPOUND	FREE SPACE	RESIGNATION	MALICE
TRANSIENTS	BAITING	STOLID	EULOGY	DESECRATING
PERSEVERANCE	REFRACTED	SUPPLICATION	USURPER	INCREDULOUS

Their Eyes Were Watching God V

SULTRY	DISGORGED	DWINDLED	SAUNTERED	SACRILEGE
WANTON	LACERATING	JURISDICTION	FEND	FEROCITY
FRACAS	MIEN	FREE SPACE	HYPOCRITES	VELOCITY
ENDURABLE	TEMPORIZED	BROACHED	COMPELLMENT	INSINUATIONS
DELIRIUM	SUBMISSION	GAPED	FETID	GALLANTLY

www.ingramcontent.com/pod-product-compliance
Lightning Source LLC
Chambersburg PA
CBHW081455070526
44586CB00019B/2365